Toward a Chican@ Hip Hop Anti-colonialism

Toward a Chican@ Hip Hop Anti-colonialism makes visible the anti-colonial, alterNative politics in hip hop texts created by Chican@s and Xican@s (indigenous-identified people of Mexican descent in the United States). McFarland builds on indigenous knowledge, anarchism, and transnational feminism to identify the emancipating power of Chican@ and Xican@ hip hop, including how women and non-gender conforming (two-spirit) MCs open up inclusive alterNative spaces that challenge colonialism and capitalism.

Pancho McFarland is Professor of Sociology at Chicago State University. He is the author of *The Chican@ Hip Hop Nation: Politics of a New Millennial Mestizaje* and *Chicano Rap: Gender and Violence in the Postindustrial Barrio*.

Routledge Focus on Latina/o Popular Culture

The Routledge Focus on Latina/o Popular Culture book series provides readers with a succinct overview of critical topics spanning across Latina/o studies and pop culture. Each book narrows in on important cultural moments in Latina/o history and media, serving as a short, detailed introduction to pressing issues intersecting between Latina/o and pop culture today.

Toward a Chican@ Hip Hop Anti-colonialism

Pancho McFarland

Routledge
Taylor & Francis Group

LONDON AND NEW YORK

First published 2018
by Routledge

2 Park Square, Milton Park, Abingdon, Oxfordshire OX14 4RN
52 Vanderbilt Avenue, New York, NY 10017

Routledge is an imprint of the Taylor & Francis Group, an informa business

First issued in paperback 2019

Library of Congress Cataloging-in-Publication Data
A catalog record for this book has been requested

ISBN: 978-1-138-55189-3 (hbk)
ISBN: 978-0-367-89139-8 (pbk)

Typeset in Times New Roman
by Apex CoVantage, LLC

**For my mother and my children. In lak 'ech.
And, to all my relations.**

Contents

1 New Millennial Colonialism

Capitalism in the 21st Century

The dawning of the 21st century gave us postindustrial globalized capitalism in the United States; global burning and climate chaos; renewed migration on the part of indigenous peoples living south of the U.S.-Mexico border-lands and the violent attack against these migrants and their cultures; amplified criminalization of youth of color (internally colonized people in the United States), the War on Drugs, and mass incarceration; and the increased reliance on and ubiquity of communications and surveillance technology.

This period also gave rise to social movements responding to and over-coming oppressive forces of capitalism, colonialism, and racism. These include deep and social ecology; transnational indigenous autonomy and nationalist movements; food and environmental justice; anti-racism; Occupy; anti-globalization; GLBTQ rights; and variants of anarchism and Marxism. Each of these movements seeks freedoms from seemingly ever-more oppressive and repressive conditions of late capitalism and the hegemonic culture attending it. Participants in these and all social move-ments share unique subcultures and identities which are requisite for a suc-cessful social movement (Pulido 1994). Identities develop as a consequence of oppression and as a means of struggle. Social movement actors work hard to develop and maintain a unified resistant identity. Successful move-ments develop a worldview that resonates well with a mass public. They distribute their values, ethics, ways of thinking and other aspects of their worldview through cultural channels including art, journalism, and music.

Hip hop was birthed and nurtured at the dawning of the new millennium (McFarland 2008, 2013; Peláez Rodríguez 2016). Perhaps, it was the love child of late capitalism and the resistance to it. Or maybe it developed in order to chronicle the tensions resulting from the clash of capitalist coloni-alism against the global working class and the indigenous. What is certain is that it has united many across racial and geographic lines. Whether it contributes to oppressive, colonial forces or to the resistance to and tran-scendence of capitalism, colonialism and other systems of domination is still understudied. Ball's (2011) study of the corporate rap industry and the possibilities for emancipatory journalism through hip hop technologies remains the most useful contribution to answering the question of where hip hop can be positioned in the new millennial struggles for freedom. Following his use of a decolonial perspective, I examine how Chican@ street hop and Xican@ hip hop express an anti-authoritarian, anti-colonial, alterNative worldview through attention to place and identity. Many Chican@ emcees employee an anti-colonial and anti-capitalist aesthetics. Their discussions of identity in Chican@ hip hop reflect a continuation of maíz narratives and the pinto poet tradition. As Villa (2000) has argued, space/land is a central aspect of discussions of identity in Chican@ literature and culture. I argue that careful attention to identity through hip hop narratives of place reveals important insight about Chican@ experience, Xican@ (indigenous-identified) political activity, and the state of our nation in the new millennium. Moreover, Xican@ hip hop narratives of identity have potential for emancipatory political projects that are anti-authoritarian, anti-colonial, alterNative and pro-life or, as the Zapatistas would say, "Against Neoliberalism and For Humanity." Their rhetorical resistance against colonialism, capitalism, and authoritarianism of all stripes can inspire others to act. Yet, if they limit themselves to a 'decolonial aesthetics' and do not engage with communities in struggle on the ground their analyses and impact will suffer.

In the following I examine a set of Chican@ hip hop texts for evidence of anti-authoritarian, anti-colonial, alterNative politics. Through a synthesis of anti-colonial indigenous thought, anarchism, and transnational decolonial feminism I propose a framework by which to assess the degree to which Chican@ hip hop texts can serve an emancipatory agenda. To begin, the rest of this chapter presents the current colonial capitalist crises facing Chican@s. I focus on contemporary capitalist tactics of the War on Drugs and the ongoing criminalization of people of Mexican descent, the role of the mass media and public education in normalizing the racist capitalist status quo, and gendered colonial practices that undermine all people of Mexican descent by attacking women, la jotería and gays, lesbians, bisexuals, transgenders, queers, and two-spirited (GLBTQ2) and pitting women and GLBTQ2 people against cishet men (men whose gender-identity matches their assigned birth sex and who are attracted to women).

In Chapter 2 I offer my anti-authoritarian, anti-colonial, alterNative framework. My perspective borrows from alterNative theorists Alicia Gaspar de Alba (1998) and Devon G. Peña (2014). I utilize the indigenist anarchist theorizing of Taiaike Alfred (2009, 2005) and other revolutionary anti-colonial indigenous scholarship. My theoretical perspective relies on the transnational feminist theories of Emma Perez (1999, 1990) and Rita Dhamon (2015) and anarchist feminism. They practice a third space

feminism that pushes back against masculinist anti-colonial and revolutionary work while offering new perspectives on resistance to colonialism, anti-
capitalism, and alterNative futures. The anarchism of Kropotkin, Malatesta,
Flores Magón, and others adds a relentless and multifaceted critique of
capitalism and the European-style nation-state. Moreover, queer indigenous studies and jotería studies offer keen insight into how colonialism
and capitalism use sexuality and sexual difference as weapons to subjugate
the colonized, racialized, and working classes; how subordinated groups
and nations often succumb to the colonizer's gender/sex/sexuality system;
and how a two-spirited or jot@ analysis is central to anti-colonial projects.

The next two chapters apply my alterNative framework to the new millennial maíz narratives of Xican@ (Chican@ indigenous, Mexica) hip hop and
the pinto poetry of Chican@ street hop. Chapter 3 examines place and identity in Xican@ hip hop and how Xican@ emcees develop an anti-colonial
aesthetics employing a rhetorical reclamation of land/space and indigeneity
that connect Xican@s of the 21st century urban United States with our indigenous elders and ancestors. That Xican@ emcees struggle for and promote
indigenous ways of being, seeing, and understanding means that they would
oppose colonialism, capitalism, and private property. I examine the degree
to which they express and embody these struggles. Chapter 4 presents Chi-
can@ street hop as a continuation of the pinto poet tradition in Chican@
culture. The "aggressive insubordination" or "menace" (Tinajero 2016) of
Chicano street hop critiques capitalism and colonialism and reterritorial-
izes urban space. They engage in an identity-shaping process that redefines
people of Mexican descent and resituates them as revolutionary subjects.
While often prescient in their analyses of colonialism and capitalism in
the new millennium, the revolutionary possibility of both Xicano (male)
hip hop and Chicano (male) street hop is limited since women's voices are
largely absent and the representations of women are limited to stereotypes.
Moreover, sexuality other than hypermasculine conquest narratives rarely
enter into rap narratives of men of Mexican descent and hostility towards
members of the GLBTQ2 population is not uncommon. Patriarchal colonial
capitalist hypermasculinity can have no place in an anti-colonial, alterNative society. Fortunately, Xicanas open a third space in hip hop. Throughout
the two chapters I describe and analyze Xicana hip hop texts. I examine
their challenge to Chicano hip hop, masculine anti-colonial analysis, and
the reclamation of indigeneity.

I conclude the study with final thoughts on the emancipatory possibilities
of Chican@ hip hop and how we might expand the Xican@ anti-colonial
hip hop analysis. I present the strengths, weaknesses and promise of an
anti-authoritarian, anti-colonial, alterNative Xican@ hip hop. I offer to the
reader and the listener a way of thinking about the potential contributions

of hip hop to revolutionary consciousness and praxis and where Xican@ hip hop falls short of a liberatory politics. In addition, I suggest further avenues of intellectual inquiry that can lead to an anti-authoritarian, alter-Native future.

Colonialism, Capitalism, and the War on Drugs

Scholarly analyses of Chican@ culture commonly begin with the Spanish invasion of Mexico in 1519 and emphasize the period after U.S. conquest of Mexico's northwestern territories in 1848. Xican@ (persons of Mexican descent in the United States who identify as indigenous)[1] analyses start a few thousand years earlier. These anti-colonial, alterNative analyses challenge taken-for-granted assumptions about Mexican peoples in the United States as foreigners, illegals, and 'mixed-raced'. Like the Chican@ cultural renaissance of the 1960s and 1970s Xican@ analyses situate Chican@ identity and culture within a much longer span of history and an indigenous civilizational milieu that spans Abya Yala (the Americas) (Peña 2005; Pilcher 1998; Rodriguez 2015).

Anti-colonial, alterNative analyses pose a challenge not only to liberal academic historiography but also to progressive critiques that similarly view Chican@ marginalization, exploitation, and disenfranchisement as a result of a highly stratified U.S. social system. Whereas class-based Marxist analyses emphasize capitalism as the culprit and many others argue that racism causes Chican@ suffering, alterNative perspectives locate the roots of current injustice with colonialism. Contrary to much academic writing, we are not in a post-colonial era. Indigenous peoples including Chican@s continue to be dispossessed of their cultures, territories, and lives through an intricate web of local, national and international law, police and military violence, racist media campaigns, and poverty. Importantly, the current neoliberal economic regime relies on free trade agreements/practices and the War on Drugs to accumulate indigenous/Mexican/Chican@ territory and control working-class and indigenous Chican@s/Mexican@s.

Colonial dispossession of land in Abya Yala caused and continues to cause the proletarianization of indigenous/Chican@ people. With Chican@/indigenous people displaced from their land and their thousands-years-old collective place-based culture, colonial authorities enforce social control. Racial terror, law enforcement, segregation, and other mechanisms have forced Chican@s into working-class barrios besieged by the problems that result from impoverishment including violence, unemployment, disease, drugs, crime, and psychological challenges. Without land Chican@s must survive as workers in fields and factories replete with low pay, instability, and workplace hazards. Following Villa (2000, 4) I refer to this 'complex of dominating social processes' and outcomes experienced by many Chican@s as 'barrioization'—the predominant form that colonialism takes for people of Mexican descent in the United States. Throughout the 20th century most Chican@s found themselves attempting to live a dignified life under oppressive conditions. Importantly, Chican@s have utilized expressive culture and place-making strategies as means of dignified struggle (Villa 2000; Peña 2005). Chican@s develop a barriology using song, dance, art, literature, and horticulture to remember place and culture and to reterritorialize space and redefine identity (Alvarez 2008; Peña 2005; Villa 2000; Zibechi 2012).

While Chican@s attempt to live lives of dignity and to prosper in the United States, the forces of capital and the State continuously reorganize and rely on new tactics to control this racialized proletarianized indigenous people. The 1970s and 1980s brought two important new yet familiar tactics: neo-liberal economic strategies and the War on Drugs. The capitalist economic and social system reached a new phase at the end of the 20th century. As a result of challenges by the oppressed and marginalized throughout the world in the 1960s, ruling elites restructured global economics through neo-liberal globalization. Corporate bosses reshaped international law to allow easier access to foreign markets and labor. As manufacturing became internationalized the United States deindustrialized. Well-paid manufacturing work that allowed many people of color to escape absolute poverty after World War II crossed our national borders and became superexploitive in underdeveloped colonial nations. In Mexico multinational corporations gobbled land and resources, leaving Mexican workers without opportunities to thrive or even survive. This new economic order and policies, especially the North American Free Trade Agreement/Tratado de Libre Comercio, led directly to the mass exodus of millions of Mexicans to the United States. Under the neo-liberal economy Chican@s saw their livelihoods attacked and their communities left in ruins as factories that helped stabilize neighborhoods closed down, leaving empty streets and the underground economy. The era of economic restructuring beginning in the 1980s shifted the tax burden to working people, replaced workers with machines, undermined union power, and shifted government spending priorities from human capital to war. The effects of this urban devastation resulted in many Chican@s participating in the informal economy while some engaged in the illicit or criminal economy that further destabilizes communities.

Nixon and the ruling elites created the "War on Drugs" as a means to contain working-class people of color and to roll back the gains of the Civil Rights Movement and working-class revolution of the 1960s and 1970s. This 'war' structures many of the experiences of urban Chican@ working-class youth. The conclusions that Michelle Alexander draws regarding the heavy toll that the "War on Drugs" has had on Black men and Black communities can be applied to understanding many Chican@ communities. Alexander (2012, 98) offers a telling statistic about "Latino" incarceration rates. She points out that from 1983 to 2000 the number of Latin@ prison admissions for drug cases increased more than twenty-fold! She explains (Alexander 2012, 40–58) that political and media scare tactics, politicians' desires to capture the white working-class vote, 'tough on crime' legislation, and the consequences of deindustrialization led to the "War on Drugs," which has had enormous negative consequences for Black and Latin@ communities. Mass incarceration of Chican@ men has led to their extreme marginalization, disenfranchisement, and second-class citizen status. Jose Luis Morin reports that the "War on Drugs" "is in fact the single greatest force behind the growth of the prison population of Latinos in prisons around the United States. This war on drugs is almost entirely being fought in Latino and African American communities" (quoted in Anonymous 2010). State prison populations at the time sharpen Morin's point. In 2010 the number of persons incarcerated per 100,000 persons were as follows: White men, 380; Latino men, 966; Black men, 2,207 (Prison Policy Initiative n.d.). Similarly, 34.2% of federal prisoners identified as Hispanic in May 2015 (Bureau of Prisons 2015).

Colonialism, deindustrialization, racism, the War on Drugs and the media and other ideological state apparatuses have barrioized, impoverished, and deterritorialized working-class Chican@ youth. These conditions have led many Chican@s to express their experiences through hip hop tales and actions that reflect, sometimes celebrate, and other times critique their situations in the urban United States during the beginning of the new millennium. In addition, many Xican@s use hip hop to reclaim identity and reterritorialize their urban environs. Such cultural expression reflects the legacies of maíz narratives and pinto poetics as stories of resistance and recovery.

Ideology: Mass Media and Education

Colonialism and capitalism along with many other forms of domination work through ideology. The 'logic of coloniality' (Cervantes and Saldaña 2015) in the United States requires the image of the savage, uncivilized, undeserving native. Theorizing how Chican@s and other indigenous Americans 'disrupt savagism', Arturo Aldama (2001, 17) quotes Tejaswini Niranjana, who wrote: "By colonial discourse I mean the body of knowledge, modes of representation, strategies of power, law, discipline, and so on, that are employed in the construction and domination of 'colonial subjects.'" To further the colonial goals of the material dispossession of indigenous people, European colonizers created the 'savage' who "exists outside of any human cultivation" (Aldama 2001, 10). The colonizer required 'epistemic violence' in order to "rationalize the material violence committed on the bodies of these colonial subjects" (Aldama 2001, 17). The ideology of European supremacy and civilization and the power and privileges it has bestowed upon elites of European-descent required that indigenous people be seen as inferior savages. The continued exploitation and dispossession of native and Chican@ resources requires a similar colonial trope of Chican@/native incivility and Otherness. Contemporary colonialism and capitalism use mass media and education to inculcate the logics of coloniality. They are the primary disseminators of the colonial discourse and use 'hip hop' to extend it to the masses of youth of color.

Under colonialism and capitalism ideology functions to shape culture for the purposes of maintaining social order especially through controlling information and providing the limitations on the popular discourse. Further, I concur with Jared A. Ball's (2011, 13) analysis that "mass media, the function of which is always the maintenance or expansion of that national ideology, are today more pervasive, more powerful, and more tightly controlled than at any other point in world history." Media consolidation has created a situation in which only four media corporations (Sony, Universal Music Group, Warner Music Group, and EMI) control 95% of the compact discs "sold in the Western world" (Ball 2011, 72). Other media including radio, television, book and magazine publishing, and movies are similarly concentrated. The Telecommunications of Act of 1996 allowed for an unprecedented concentration of communication and information so that today 90% of media companies are owned by just six transnational corporations: Disney, Time Warner, Viacom, Comcast, CBS, and News Corporation (Corcoran 2016).

The media engages in psychic violence against colonized people of color (Ball 2011, 13). Undermining the emotions, spirit, and understanding of the colonized the 'fourth arm of the military' (mass media) enhances the military and police use of physical violence and threat. The pervasiveness of the media in the seat of empire and its control by a small number of ruling-class elites means that the colonized see images that are pro-capital, pro-consumerist, anti-Mexicano, and anti-indigenous. To be a rightful citizen of the empire is to deny indigenous, Mexican, alterNative culture and to adopt a pro-capitalist consumerist mentality. Media encourages us to abandon and denigrate the traditions of our ancestors for consumerist ethics and behavior. The colonized learn to define ourselves through media images and the products that we consume rather than the pro-life indigenous value systems of our people. "Latin@" identity works in this way. 'Latino' and 'Latina' deny indigeneity through their etymological ties to Europe instead of Abya Yala effectively erasing the indigenous and the African (McFarland

2013; McFarland and Ball 2016). Through corporate commodified reggaeton music, media companies mold a euro-derived capitalist, consumerist Latin@. Ball (2011, 33) warns that an additional effect of mass media saturation "continues to be an audience predominantly incapable of interpreting our reality, organizing to change it, or with an outlet to promote the need and existence of that resistance." However, like in hip hop, Latin@ youth involved with reggaeton resist the logics of coloniality through their expression of identity (McFarland 2013).[2]

The mass media including and especially radio and television provide a limited number of ways of being Mexicana, Chicano, or indigenous. Media consolidation and power allows for "the popularization of only certain forms of colonized culture, which support the larger project of the colonizers (who of course are in command of that popularization process)" (Ball 2011, 43). The mass media provide few images of indigenous people and a limited range of possibilities for being Mexicano or Latina: thugs, illegal immigrants, uneducated, impoverished workers. Chicanos are depicted as violent on the big and small screens and popular reggaeton music offers 'Latin@' hypersexuality and consumerism. Radio station playlists include only a very few non-threatening songs played in heavy rotation so that it is common to hear the same songs and artists reinforcing capitalist, colonialist stereotypes of 'Latin@s' several times in an hour.

Veteran Chicano street hop emcee, Kemo the Blaxican, offers his critique of the music industry on "2010 Ignorant" (2010) in which he takes on the personae of a typical popular rapper. He says, "every time I tune the radio/another song of blunts, riches and hoes." He argues that to have radio success an emcee or rapper must record lyrics that deal with illicit drugs (blunts), money (riches), and sexualized women (hoes). Like Ball and other media critics, Kemo suggests that only those deemed acceptable by the media elite or that support racist stereotypes are allowed to become popular. With few critical-thinking skills and limited ability to ask questions and seek out information on their own, young people especially are vulnerable to such media manipulation. The education system provides young people few opportunities to develop free, creative inquiry and, thus, serves an important ideological function for capitalism and colonialism.

Resistant street hop discussed later often challenges education in the United States by pointing out its collusion with the colonial project or, as the pan-African, pro-working class duo, Dead Prez (2000) argues, "Schools don't teach us shit/white man lies straight bullshit." Segregated schools, tracking, educational impoverishment in inner cities and rural areas, and emphasis on discipline, rote memorization, and following orders limits the ability of students from colonized groups to think creatively, outside the parameters of accepted discourse, and in their own interests. In his lecture, "40 Years of Hip Hop," veteran emcee, activist, and hip hop scholar KRS-One describes public education today: "Public education doesn't inspire you . . . public education is for you to respond reflexively to authority . . . 'When I say 'jump'. You say, 'How high?' That's it. Nothing about your culture."

From the anti-colonial alterNative perspective the content of colonial classrooms is Eurocentric and aggressively invisibilizes Chican@ indigeneity. Krazy Race, Chicano street hop artist, raps on "Dedicated" (2004):

> As I'm sitting in class they're trying to teach me European./I'm listening to a voice/but I represent the bean/eating population/founders of cultivation/people of the Sun/mighty Brown nation/who've been suppressed and held down for many long years./My face drops a tear/as your pale people cheer./The time is near/and yet you celebrate the hate/days of genocide where my kind was robbed and raped./In 1521 we were slaughtered by the thousands/now in 2000/we're still living in project housing./Something for you to think about./Krazy Race is in the house/about to turn the lights out.

Krazy Race offers an alterNative street hop analysis of the ideological functions of public education and an alterNative Xican@ identity. In his alterNative worldview, people of Mexican descent are powerful and ingenious. Moreover, the weak, ineffectual Mexican promoted by schools and the media is not the cause of Chican@ crime, poverty, poor housing, and other urban social problems. Rather, 500 years of colonialism and genocide has resulted in contemporary poverty in which many are relegated to 'project housing'.

On their 2006 compact disc, *E.S.L.*, Akwid[3] provides an insightful critique of the education system and recuperation of Chican@/Mexican@ identity. Throughout the compact disc Akwid presents skits that make fun of the English-as-a-Second-Language instruction that many young Mexican@s experience in colonial U.S. schools. Akwid depicts ESL instructors as completely misunderstanding Mexican@ students. Instructors offer racist stereotypes about their clothes, language, and culture. The skits illustrate the foolishness and ignorance of the presumably white instructors. They turn the tables on the racist stereotypes and the white colonial agent becomes the ineffectual and the idiotic. They resist the gangbanger image that these instructors hold of them and loudly claim resistance and resilience. In the opening song, "El Principio", over distinctly Mexican instrumentation using a tuba to perform the bass parts and trumpets adding flare a la banda music, they proudly chant the chorus "you can take me out the hood but you can't take the hood out of me cuz I'mma be where I come from" and say later that they are "puro Mexicano cien porciento" (one hundred percent pure Mexican). Theirs is a place-based ('hood') and Mexican@ working-class reclamation of Mexican diasporic identity from racist settler media and public education and a young, 1.5 generation hip hop redefinition of who we are.

Chican@ street hop and indigenous-focused hip hop develop a resurgent, resistant alterNative identity that challenges the spirit-crushing attacks by the colonial capitalist media and education system. Groups and solo artists such as Krazy Race, Akwid, Kemo the Blaxican, and others discussed in the following chapters open a space in which young people can challenge capitalism, colonialism, and racism and re-create new millennial identities rooted in ancestral tradition, revolutionary left analysis and action, and a polycultural world that allows them to borrow the best of resistant Black cultural production and communist and anarchist class analysis (McFarland 2013). While narrative space is opened to reclaim and redefine, often due to the insidious nature of colonial capitalist ideology and to the fact that hip hop culture is masculinized, women are marginalized, commodified, Othered, and attacked. In the chapters that follow I analyze the degree to which the resistant hip hop of Xicanos and street hop emcees has room for a third space transnational feminist praxis that offers visions for a truly free future.

The Gendered Colonial System

Colonialism, capitalism, and other forms of domination require a divide-and-conquer strategy; a separation of the colonized, working class, or other dominated group into rival sectors. Colonialism and capitalism use xenophobic nationalism, racism, and sexism as tools of division. Patriarchal systems pit men against women and different groups of women against each other. Thus it follows that attention to racism without concern for how sexism and racism reinforce one another inevitably fails at ending racism and creating an alterNative future. Black feminist scholar, Patricia Hill Collins (2004, 7), summarizes this point concerning Black sexual politics writing that "racism is a gender-specific phenomenon, and Black antiracist politics that do not make gender central are doomed to fail because someone will always be left behind. If either women or men remain subordinated, then social injustice persists." To address the gendered racist colonial gaze, feminists suggest an intersectional politics that "view race, class, gender, sexuality, ethnicity, and age, among others as mutually constructing systems of power" (Collins 2004, 11).

Colonialism and capitalism attack women in numerous ways. Bañales (2014, 159) sums up the strategy of the colonial capitalist system, writing "the colonization of the Americas imposed a Eurocentric gender system" and utilized gender/sexual violence. The policing and punishing of women's bodies goes hand-in-glove with capitalist colonialism. Laws and cultural practices strip women of bodily autonomy and promise colonized men the possibility of the control of "their" women's bodies. Examining the history of Spanish Catholic missions as a colonizing institution, Antonia I. Castañeda (1993, 25) addresses the legal and acceptable practice of the rape of indigenous women in California. She summarizes the use of rape, writing "rape is an act of domination, an act of power. As such, it is a violent political act committed through sexual aggression against women." The colonial white supremacist system established in Mexico and the United States dominated and continues to dominate indigenous people through the threat of sexual violence. The European Christian colonizers imposed their binary gender system upon native people using sexual and other violence, boarding schools, and rewards for displays of loyalty to the colonial (gender) system. The result has been that colonized and racialized peoples in the United States have internalized colonial sexism and accepted patriarchal understandings of men, women, and the family. Emma Pérez (1990, 63) argues convincingly that colonized Chicanos "absorb the white colonizer-father's ways [and] hierarchically impose them on Chicanas, becoming caricatures of the white colonizer-father." This system has endured for 500 years with slight modifications. Thus, it is no wonder that colonized and racialized men including Chicanos reproduce the ideology in their actions and popular culture including hip hop (McFarland 2008).

Along with violence against Indigenous women, colonial systems use heteropatriarchy and heteronormativity to undermine Indigenous people. Arguing for Indigenous sovereignty, Driskill, Finley, Gilley and Morgensen (2011, 8) write "that decolonization for Indigenous people will follow declaring sovereignty from the heteropatriarchal politics, economics, and cultures inherited from colonization." Colonial projects including Catholic missions and boarding schools indoctrinated and assimilated natives into a euro heteropatriarchal worldview that included the nuclear family, heteronormativity, man as the head of the household, and obedience to male and white authority. Sovereignty seeks freedom from such colonial modes of thought and being.

Today's proponents of the new racism use gender in renewed but familiar ways. Collins shows how racism changes to meet changing political economic conditions. A postindustrial neo-liberal capitalism in the multicultural United States at the dawn of the new millennium requires slight modifications in the gendered racist colonial system. Collins's (2004, 1990) concept 'controlling images' proves useful for the purposes of analyzing popular culture and the potential role of Xican@ hip hop in liberatory activity. Men in hip hop culture, especially the corporate version presented in popular music videos and on corporate radio stations, represent women in ways that undermine Black women and the liberation of Black people. The same could be said about how women of Mexican descent are depicted in hip hop and throughout the popular culture landscape. Collins shows how controlling images such as 'bitch', 'booty', 'ho' (whore), 'freak', and 'gold digger' replay older racist sexist images of Black women as the overly sexual and dangerous 'Jezebel' (Collins 2004, ch. four). Hip hop's misogyny mirrors and amplifies that of the larger society that sees women's bodies and beings connected to treasure, money, sex, and greed. Importantly, there is little space in hip hop for women to express their sides of the story, their view of things, and their insight into Xican@ identity, values, and cultural renewal and resistance.

The Capitalist Colonialist Matrix

The oppression, marginalization, and limits to freedom experienced by the colonized, people of color, poor, gender non-conforming, and women results from a colonial matrix of domination (Collins 1990) consisting of violence, legal regimes, ideology, and heteropatriarchy. Our freedom requires destruction of each element in the matrix and the forging of indigenous epistemologies, ontologies, ways of being, and identities. Many scholars, activists, and revolutionaries have proposed pathways to resistant indigeneity and new forms of social organization forged out of ancestral practice. In the following chapter I outline a synthesis of these pathways, which I describe as an anti-authoritarian, anti-colonial, alterNative politics.

Notes

1 I use a number of related but different spellings to refer to people of the Mesoamerican Diaspora. The group of people I discuss throughout are people of Mexican descent. We sometimes refer to people of Mexican descent in the United States as Chicanos. The sexist nature of the Spanish language has been challenged for decades and we use non-sexist versions of the word including Chicana/o and Chican@. I use Chican@ throughout to refer to both male and female people of Mexican descent in the United States. When emphasizing indigenous aspects of Chican@ life and culture I use the Chican@ indigenous spelling Xican@, Xicano (men/boys, male only) or Xicana (women/girls, female only). I also use Mexican@, Mexicano, and Mexicana when discussing people, ideas, and issues related to members of the Mesoamerican diaspora who identify as Mexican or when I emphasize the "Mexican-ness" of a particular aspect of culture or history.
2 For a more thorough analysis of the reggaeton industry and Latin@ identity see ch. eight, "'Soy la Kalle': Radio, Reggaeton and Latin@ Identity," in my book, *The Chican@ Hip Hop Nation: Politics of a New Millennial Mestizaje* (2013).
3 See ch, four, pages 103–111, of my book, *The Chican@ Hip Hop Nation: Politics of a New Millennial Mestizaje*, for a more thorough discussion of Akwid's work.

Bibliography

Akwid. 2006. E.S.L. (album). Univision.

Aldama, Arturo. 2001. *Disrupting Savagism: Intersecting, Chicana/o, Mexican Immigrant, and Native American Struggles for Self-Representation*. Durham, NC: Duke University Press.

Alexander, Michelle. 2012. *The New Jim Crow: Mass Incarceration in the Age of Colorblindness*. New York: The New Press.

Alfred, Taiaike. 2009. *Peace, Power, Righteousness: An Indigenous Manifesto*. Oxford: Oxford University Press.

———. 2005. *Wasase: Indigenous Pathways of Action and Freedom*. Petersborough, ON: Broadview Press.

Alvarez, Luis. 2008. *The Power of the Zoot: Youth Culture and Resistance During World War II*. Berkeley: University of California Press.

Anonymous. 2010. "Criminal Justice: Inequities for Latinos in Criminal Justice." Young Latino Male Symposium. W.W. Kellogg Foundation. September. http://cronkitezine.asu.edu/latinomales/criminal.html

Ball, Jared A. 2011. *I Mix What I Like: A Mixtape Manifesto*. Oakland, CA: AK Press.

Bañales, Xamuel. 2014. "Jotería: A Decolonizing Political Project." *Aztlán: A Journal of Chicano Studies*. 39:1: 155–165.

Bureau of Prisons. 2015. "Inmate Ethnicity." www.bop.gov/about/statistics/statistics_inmate_ethnicity.jsp

Castañeda, Antonia I. 1993. "Sexual Violence in the Politics and Policies of Conquet: Amerindian Women and the Spanish Conquest of Alta California." In de la Torre, A. and B. M. Pesquera (eds.). *Building with Our Hands: New Directions in Chicana Studies*. Berkeley, CA: University of California Press. Pp. 15–33.

Cervantes, Marco Antonio and Lilliana Patricia Saldaña. 2015. "Hip Hop and Nueva Cancion as Decolonial Pedagogies of Epistemic Justice." *Decolonization: Indigeneity, Education and Society*. 4:1.

Collins, Patricia Hill. 2004. *Black Sexual Politics: African Americans, Gender, and the New Racism*. New York: Routledge.

———. 1990. *Black Feminist Thought: Knowledge, Consciousness, and the Politics of Empowerment*. Cambridge, MA: Unwin Hyman.

Corcoran, M. 2016. "20 Years of Media Consolidation Has Not Been Good for Our Democracy." March 30. Moyer's and Company. http://billmoyers.com/story/twenty-years-of-media-consolidation-has-not-been-good-for-our-democracy/

Dead Prez. 2000. "They Schools." *Let's Get Free*. Loud Music.

Dhamon, Rita. 2015. "A Feminist Approach to Decolonizing Anti-Racism: Rethinking Transnationalism, Intersectionality and Settler Colonialism." *Feral Feminisms*. 4: 20–37.

Driskill, Qwo-Li, Chris Finley, Brian J. Gilley and Scott Lauria Morgensen (eds.). 2011. *Queer Indigenous Studies: Critical Interventions in Theory, Politics, and Literature*. Tucson: University of Arizona Press.

Gaspar de Alba, Alicia. 1998. *Chicano Art Inside/Outside the Master's House: Cultural Politics and the CARA Exhibition*. University of Texas Press.

Kemo the Blaxican. 2010. "2010 Ignorant." *Upside of Struggle*. Dead Silence Records.

Krazy Race. 2004. "Dedicated."

KRS-One. 2015. "40 Years of Hip Hop by KRS-One." www.youtube.com/watch?v=REpSdgORU5A

McFarland, Pancho. 2013. *The Chican@ Hip Hop Nation: Politics of a New Millennial Mestizaje*. East Lansing: Michigan State University Press.

———. 2008. *Chicano Rap: Gender and Violence in the Postindustrial Barrio*. Austin: University of Texas Press.

——— and Jared A. Ball. 2016. "Ya Basta! Con Latino!: The Re-Indigenization and Re-Africanization of Hip Hop." In Castillo-Garcow, Melissa and Jason Nichols (eds.). *La Verdad: An International Dialogue on Hip Hop Latinidades*. Columbus, OH: Ohio State University Press. Pp. 41-59

Peláez Rodríguez, Diana C. 2016. "Chicana Hip Hop: Expanding Knowledge in the L.A. Barrio." In Castillo-Garsow, Melissa and Jason Nichols (eds.). *La Verdad: An International Dialogue on Hip Hop Latinidades*. Columbus: Ohio State University Press. Pp. 183–202.

Peña, Devon G. 2014. "Revolutions Happen: Notes on the Crisis of Neoliberalism and the Subversiveness of the Common." April 18. Ejfood.blogspot.com.

———. 2005. *Mexican Americans and the Environment*. Tucson: University of Arizona Press.

Perez, Emma. 1999. *The Decolonial Imaginary: Writing Chicanas into History*. Bloomington, IN: Indiana University Press.

———. 1990. "Speaking from the Margin: Uninvited Discourse on Sexuality and Power." In de la Torre, Adela and Beatriz M. Pesquera (eds.). *Building with Our Hands: New Directions in Chicana Studies*. Berkeley, CA: University of California Press. Pp. 57–71.

Pilcher, Jeffrey M. 1998. *Que Vivan Los Tamales! Food and the Making of Mexican Identity*. Albuquerque: University of New Mexico Press.

Prison Policy Initiative. N.d. "United States Incarceration Rates." www.prisonpolicy.org/graphs/raceinc.html

Pulido, Laura. 1994. "Development of the People of Color Identity in the Environmental Justice Movement of the Southwestern United States." *Socialist Review*. 26:3–4: 145–180.

Rodriguez, Robert C. 2015. *Our Sacred Maíz Is Our Mother: Indigeneity and Belonging in the Americas*. Tucson: University of Arizona Press.

Tinajero, Robert. 2016. "Borderland Hip Hop Rhetoric: Identity and Counterhegemony." In Castillo-Garsow, Melissa and Jason Nichols (eds.). *La Verdad: An International Dialogue on Hip Hop Latinidades*. Columbus: Ohio State University Press. Pp. 17–40.

Villa, Raul Homero. 2000. *Barrio Logos: Space and Place in Urban Chicano Literature and Culture*. Austin: University of Texas Press.

Zibechi, Raul. 2012. *Territories in Resistance: A Cartography of Latin American Social Movements*. Oakland, CA: AK Press.

2 Anti-authoritarian, Anti-colonial, AlterNative Politics

According to George Jackson "the job of the revolutionary in reactionary times is to make space for revolution to occur" (quoted in Ball 2011, 127). Through examining race, place, and gender in Xican@ hip hop and street hop I illustrate how some in this cultural movement perform this revolutionary function. Such performance pedagogies can provide hip hop headz and listeners with opportunities "to critique and delink from coloniality in their everyday lives" (Cervantes and Saldaña 2015, 86). Xican@ hip hop and street hop operationalize a decolonial imaginary, becoming sites for 'rethink[ing] history in a way that makes Chicana/o agency transformative' (Perez 1999, 5). If, as discussed earlier, colonialism works both through material and ideological means, then hip hop struggle (both over the meaning of hip hop and how Xican@s use it as a tool in the decolonizing process) is crucial to anti-authoritarian, anti-colonial, alterNative politics. Obviously, any anti-colonial alterNative praxis would attack patriarchal domination, misogyny, and gender/sex inequities and root it out of decolonial activism and cultural production. Hip Hop as an alterNative liberatory cultural praxis must include a third space transnational feminism; one that is "within and between dominant male discourse" (Perez, 32) as well as a strident critique of class, race, and colonialism.

I provide a way of seeing the revolutionary potential of the new pinto poetry and maíz narratives in Xican@ hip hop and offer a critique of the how Chican@ street hop and indigenous identities in hip hop can be martialed to ideologically challenge colonialism, capitalism, and misogyny. This chapter offers a political theory steeped in anti-authoritarian (anarchist, autonomist Marxist), anti-colonial, and alterNative traditions.

AlterNative Praxis

My analysis and contribution to theories of liberation and to a revolutionary praxis is an alterNative one. Alicia Gaspar de Alba (1998, 16–17) argues that "Chicano/a culture is not only an 'alter-culture' that simultaneously differs from, is changed by, and changes the dominant culture, but is also an *alter-Native culture*-an Other culture native to this specific geography." AlterNative praxis and its study begins with us, the indigenous and the colonized, as people with a history longer than that of colonialism and thus with a distinct culture apart from any relationship with the colonizer. While colonialism has, obviously, altered the cultures of the Mexican diaspora,[1] we are not simply the colonized but, also, and more importantly, we are native.

Scholar-activist-farmer, Devon G. Peña's (2014) comprehensive definition of 'alterNative' adds to my alterNative perspective, methodology, and praxis:

> I am referring to indigenous knowledge systems, an epistemology that is place-based because it arises from the ontology of becoming in place through shared memories and the knowledge common. But dislocations alter this place-based being, rupturing generations of attachment to one's homeland and ancestral common. So the Native is 'altered.' But it does not end there, that is the anti-thesis; the synthesis, or rupture, is in the ability and strategy of the altered Native to alter the circumstances of the dislocation: Our 'alterity' means that we have had to change our perspective to that of the Other, for e.g., the cosmopolitan city-dwelling Other. But this also means we alter these new spaces in order to reinhabit place; re-locate our being in place. But in the process, we also re-invent and adapt our sense of place and indigeneity as forms of oppositional consciousness.

His emphasis on Xican@ reterritorialization of urban space speaks to place, identity, and politics in Xican@ hip hop and street hop. Graffiti, claiming of space through playing loud bass-heavy music and Xican@ hip hop lyrics claim urban places and redefine Xican@ (Alvarez 2008). Colonialism in the form of ongoing land and resource enclosures by international capital continues the dislocations common to Chican@ experience within imperial states. Dislocation alters us but we resist and persist. This alterNative praxis is evident throughout Xican@ hip hop and will be explored through a select group of hip hop texts in the subsequent chapters.

Being place-based alterNative praxis and study takes on unique forms in distinct places. All begin with indigenous worldview and this is where I begin in the next section. Beyond this, the particular circumstances of my dislocation, and to a certain degree that of many of the Xican@ emcees described in this work, places me in close proximity to political theories and action based on revolutionary socialist praxis, both Marxian and anarchist. So, my alterNative analysis of Xican@ hip hop is both anti-colonial indigenous and anarchist. Taiaike Alfred (2005, 45) offers indigenous anarchism as such a theoretical perspective, writing that a new indigenous warrior ethic is needed to deal with contemporary assaults from colonial states and capitalist industries.

> The two elements that come to mind are indigenous, evoking cultural and spiritual rootedness in this land and the Onkwehonwe struggle for justice and freedom, and the political philosophy and movement that is fundamentally anti-institutional, radically democratic, and committed to taking action to force change: anarchism.

Though indigenous and anarchist traditions promise freedom, colonialism has altered the Native using patriarchy and misogyny as well as class and territory. My study of Xican@ culture and history and my place-based activism brought me face-to-face with both patriarchal anti-capitalist and patriarchal 'anti-colonial', Chicano nationalist, and Black Power activity. Xicana and African diasporan women writers and activists insist that anti-colonial activity and decolonial art must be rooted in their perspectives and experiences. Thus, many scholars, artists, and activists develop a transnational feminist praxis that constitutes a foundation upon which we can build an anti-authoritarian, anti-colonial, alterNative theory and practice. My analysis and critique of Xican@ hip hop develops from an alterNative perspective that includes indigenous anti-colonial political theory, anarchism, and transnational feminism.

Indigenous Anti-colonial Political Theory

Hip hop can and has been a site for decolonial aesthetics. According to the Transnational Decolonial Institute, decolonial aesthetics "refers to ongoing artistic projects responding and delinking from the darker side of imperial globalization. Decolonial aesthetics seeks to recognize and open options for liberating the senses." I seek to understand if and how Xican@ hip hop and street hop constitute a 'decolonizing of the mind' (Ngugi wa Thiongo 1986). The revolutionary potential of hip hop lies in its ability to challenge colonial ideology described in the previous chapter and offer a model of organic anti-colonial thinking for young Chican@s. Indigenous anti-colonial theory provides a standard for any anti-colonial hip hop analysis and praxis.

In response to hundreds of years of colonialism, indigenous nationalists, radicals, and scholars developed a decolonial political theory and practice that generally included resistance to colonial ways and a recuperation of indigenous identity, consciousness, and mode of life based on the First Principles or Original Instructions. Indigenous anti-colonial politics is based on an Indigenous identity grounded in an indigenous mode of life. This mode of life includes the following: 'a life on/with the land that stressed individual autonomy, collective responsibility, nonhierarchical authority, communal land tenure, and mutual aid" (Coulthard 2014, 65).

Indigenous decolonialism understands the United States, Canada, and other nation-states of Abya Yala to be settler-colonial states that conquered indigenous territory, killed or removed native peoples, and replaced them with a foreign settler population whose survival in the new territory required the assistance, military and fiscal, of the settler state. Settler colonialism is established on an economic base of land theft and extractive capitalism and an ideological superstructure of white supremacy and Christianity. The indigenous that survived were shunted onto foreign lands called reservations and forced to change their modes of life. Decolonialism, then, would require dissolution of the concept of private property and the ownership of Earth, dismantling of the State, destruction of white supremacy, and return to indigenous (land-based) worldviews, epistemologies, ontologies, cosmologies, and means of governing and survival.

Indigenous worldview begins with examination of land/nature. From it we learn how to be in the world. The Anishinaabe concept 'akinoomaage' ('let the land guide') exemplifies this pan-indigenous principle. When we let land guide us we learn key modes of being reflected in indigenous concepts of respect, reciprocity, and relationships that are interdependent and mutually beneficial (Simpson 2014). Indigenous concepts such as mitakuye oyasin (all my relations) from the Lakota tradition exemplify interdependence amongst all beings while in lak 'ech (you are my other me) from the Lacandon Maya tradition suggests a respect developed as a result of recognizing the other in oneself. The indigenous of the Northwestern United States among others practice the reciprocal economic and social relations of potlach. Such principles and the governing/decision-making strategies of native peoples provide an anti-colonial alterNative social organizational model that challenges the illegitimate authority of capital and the State.

Transnational Xicana Feminism

A transnational feminist perspective must be central to any anti-authoritarian, anti-colonial alterNative political and social theory. Often in male-dominated 'revolutionary spaces' the questions of gender, gender roles, gender inequality, misogyny, homophobia, patriarchy, and women's views of colonialism, nationalism, and decolonization are only weakly broached and generally seen as secondary to class, race, and land. Rita Dhamon (2015) describes transnational feminism as form of feminism by non-elites; encompassing a multiplicity of feminisms; critical of the nation as defined in patriarchal and masculinist culture and politics; and historically specific. This transnational feminism fits well with anarchist and indigenous social theory and practice, as each rests on similar ideas. Transnational feminism argues that decolonizing practices must recognize the specificity of the conditions of the decolonizing people and place. It argues for a context-specific struggle including a self-reflexive analysis in which we understand our places within the complex matrix of colonial society and relationships. Any struggle for liberation must recognize where we act in the interests of colonialism. Settler complicity can even afflict people of color whose own struggles for civil and human rights are often based on attaining more of the resources that colonialism extracts from indigenous people. Petit bourgeois aspirations of elite people of color lead some to act on behalf of colonial masters. This comprador class always arises under colonial conditions as a means to subdue native unrest. Similarly, masculine privilege accrues even to native men who believe they benefit from complying with the colonizer's assault on native women. That many anti-colonial revolutionaries and revolutionary anarchists and communists act to suppress women's voices and perspectives or subscribe to narrow roles for women and 'natural' distinctions between men and women illustrate the point that not all anti-colonial or anti-authoritarian struggles are reflexive enough to recognize their sexist behaviors and perspectives.

African diasporan and indigenous/Chicana feminism provide important insight for developing anti-colonial alterNative frameworks. The concept 'intersectionality' helps us understand more fully that "all forms of subjugation and domination are integrally related to one another and that striving for an end of any form of oppression necessitates struggling to end all oppressions" (Lazar 2016, 38). While indigenous anti-colonial, Chicano radical, and anarchist politics inherently recognize the complexity of the interlocking oppressions of race, class, gender, and sexuality, their dominance by men has meant that more nuanced and thorough analyses stemming from women's experiences are hidden or deemed secondary to the more central problems of class, land, or race. In addition, the preferred solutions to the problems we encounter from racism, capitalism, and colonialism result from male experience and standpoint.

Revolutionary movements have been plagued by this male chauvinism and domination. Chicana, Black, and indigenous feminists and anarcha-feminists have analyzed and theorized this problem and have been at the forefront of developing a more thorough and integrated revolutionary praxis. Laura Hall (2016, 82) argues that indigenous anti-colonialism is a "gendered and ecological undoing of settler-colonial society and the colonial state." Recognizing this need to center women, land, all our relations, and GLBTQ2 people will allow for us to better approach decolonizing efforts including the reordering of society. Such an approach allows us to see not only capitalism, racism, or misogyny as the central problems of our time but also colonialism, industrialism, and the attack on all life. Moreover, the flexibility, fluidity, and situatedness of indigenous thought challenges the universalist assumptions of Marxist, anarchist, and other revolutionary praxis. Marxism conceives of a unified revolutionary working-class subject. This narrow definition of 'revolutionary subject' limits other ways of approaching social problems and revolution. Anarchists have traditionally been better at recognizing the importance of difference and developing a theory and praxis that takes difference into account but anarchist history shows that class struggle and white men's voices are often prioritized. The 'ecological embeddedness' of indigenous thought (Hall 2016, 84) makes it more flexible and adaptable to unique and changing circumstances. A context-specific feminism recognizes that most indigenous peoples of North America built social systems on egalitarian gender relations, matrilineality, and mutual respect between men, women, and all our relations (Jaimes and Halsey 1992; Gutiérrez 1991). It takes into account how people actually live their lives and how diversity, including and especially gender diversity, is key to any non-hierarchical, non-exploitive system.

The history of women of the Mexican/Mesoamerican diaspora reveals a need to apply a transnational Xicana feminist perspective to analyses of Xican@ and street hop. History, both colonial and patriarchal Chicano nationalist, leave out the voices and visions of colonized indigenous women. Emma Perez (1999, xv) argues convincingly that Xicanas "are spoken about, spoken for, and ultimately encoded as whining, hysterical, irrational, or passive women who cannot know what is good for us, who cannot know how to express or authorize our own narratives." Her *Decolonial Imaginary* presents an oppositional methodology whereby Chicana and Mexicana voices are privileged and utilized to develop a more complete understanding of Chican@/Mexican@ history. An anti-colonial hip hop praxis would pick up the lead of Perez and that of the transnational Mexicanas/Chican@s she discusses and open third spaces for critique of the anti-colonial, anti-capitalist projects of Xican@ hip hop and street hop.

As Perez (1999, 73) and many others have pointed out about nationalist, anarchist, and Marxist liberation movements and other revolutionary behavior, women's voice, perspectives, strategies, and issues were 'put on the back burner' while they focused on the more "fundamental" issues of class and nation. Revolutionary nationalist and socialist (anarchist and Marxist) theorists/activists often see sex/gender as a secondary issue. Their theories of liberation were infected with the sexist, masculinist logic of coloniality. Even so, women carved out third spaces within Mexican nationalist, revolutionary, and liberal movements. Her analysis of the women of the Partido

Liberal Mexicano (PLM) is instructive. The PLM served "as a foundation for contemporary Chicano nationalist discourse, without recognizing the PLM's transnational impetus and, where, again, Chicana activists are relegated to the margins and their history becomes the history of male activists and their priorities" (Perez 1999, 57). Thus, the PLM and its anarchist pedagogy and communication style should be kept in mind when studying Chican@ cultural production such as the hip hop examined herein since Chican@ nationalism provides the foundation for much of Xican@ hip hop politics.

Perez illustrates how the PLM, initially a liberal nationalist organization, became anarchist in 1910 based on their study of Kropotkin, Ferrer, and others. The PLM engaged in the cause of the Mexican Revolution as an anarchist organization with an internationalist pro-worker perspective. Ricardo Flores Magón, a leader and central propagandist for the PLM, displayed little care for women's issues beyond their labor and stereotypes of their feminine support role in the revolution and post-capitalist society. Perez critiques PLM's revolutionary potential, addressing their homophobia. Flores Magón and others in the PLM adopted the masculinist revolutionary rhetoric of the period. Their principles called for total emancipation for all but their practice often ignored them. Nonetheless, women used PLM's anarchist principles to open third spaces of feminist critique and expression (Perez 1999, 55–74).

Mexicanas in PLM took advantage of the rhetoric of liberation espoused by anarchists and developed an influential third space where they challenged its male supremacy. Importantly for my study of Xican@ hip hop cultural politics, the Mexicana feminists of the PLM also shared PLM's internationalism and supported it in their public statements and writings. In Perez's words (1999, 69), "The PLM women intervened interstitially, seemingly broadening the party's platform to fit their own agenda. They pleased their male party leaders, and they engaged in revolutionary activities as they saw fit." We shall see in the following chapters to what degree women in Xican@ hip hop have been able to similarly challenge colonialism and capitalism while critiquing hip hop's male supremacy and completing the male-dominated anti-colonial/revolutionary analyses and rhetoric of revolution that they espouse.

Perez shows that the Mexicana/Chicana third space feminism has always been transnational. Further, a transnational feminism attacks the masculinist colonial discourse and the nation-state. It, like anarchism and Marxism, is international and seeks social organization outside of the State. This feminism seeks a common understanding of women, decolonization, and freedom across national boundaries and links the fate of Chicanas to that of Palestinians, Lakotas, Irish, and other colonized women and men.

Transnational feminism has a great deal in common with anarchist principles including decentralization, a broad conception of power, questioning the State, acceptance of diverse means of societal organization, and the rejection of hierarchy. However, transnational feminisms do not always reject capitalism nor all forms of domination including the State and they are not always revolutionary. Moreover, anarchism while implying a drive toward ending all domination does not always practice what it preaches, as Perez and many others have pointed out. In the "Introduction" to the anarcha-feminist issue of *Perspectives on Anarchist Theory* (2016, 6) the editorial collective sums up the need for a feminist anarchism:

> An anarchist feminism is an argument that heteropatriarchy is best dismantled through a radical attack on all hierarchical systems and structures of oppression and exploitation. A feminist anarchism is an argument that the successful abolition of all hierarchical systems and structures of oppression and exploitation, requires antipatriarchal tactics, visions, means and ends. The struggle for a world without domination and injustice continues on all fronts, and when considering the full range of intersectionality, emancipation has not yet fully occurred; anarcha-feminism is needed until all these aspects have been addressed.

Within the broader anarchist milieu women have opened up third spaces challenging the heteropatriarchal perspective of revolutionaries. Anarchist women such as Emma Goldman, Voltairine De Cleyre, and Lucy Parsons and more recently the women anarchist authors in the *Perspectives* special issue and *Quiet Rumours: An Anarcha-Feminist Reader* (2012) among others have been important to challenging anarchism's masculinity and pushing it to ever-more sophisticated levels of political theorizing and activity. Additionally, women theorists of intersectionality, indigenous and Mexicana/Chicana scholar-activists, and women revolutionaries of the Global South such as the soldiers and theorists of the Zapatistas have forced anarchist men and other revolutionaries to reengage with the perspectives, strategies, and stories of women.

Two-Spirited Insight and La Jotería

The European colonialist capitalist sex/gender system is integral to subduing and undermining native peoples, communities, and cultures. Two-spirited native scholars argue convincingly that "heteronormativity . . . undermines struggles for decolonization and sovereignty and buoys the powers of colonial governance" (Driskill et al. 2011, 19). Two-spirited and jotería scholars and activists (community of GLBTQ2 people of Mexican descent) provide important insight into how colonial capitalist systems use gender, sexuality, the body, and race as central tactics in conquest. Moreover, these scholars and activists see colonialism and indigeneity from a unique standpoint that helps complete an anti-authoritarian, anti-colonial, alterNative analysis such as the one I have been describing so far and that which is required for the liberation of the indigenous, the colonized, and the racialized. The mission of the Association of Jotería Arts and Activism Scholarship explains an anti-colonial project that "envision[s] a world that affirms Jotería consciousness and that celebrates multiple pathways for generating knowledge, sharing experiences, and becoming catalysts for social change. We seek to live in a world free of all forms of ideological, institutional, interpersonal and internalized oppression" (cited in Hernandez 2016, 291).

If decolonizing requires "undoing the logic of colonization," then the logics of heteronormativity and heteropatriarchy and their uses in a racist colonialist capitalism must also be abolished (Bañales 2014, 156). Queer Indigenous Studies and two-spirited scholars and activists believe as Driskill et al. (2011) write: "decolonization for Indigenous people will follow declaring sovereignty from the heteropatriarchal politics, economics, and cultures inherited from colonization" (8). Theorizing such a decolonial project for Xican@s, Bañales (2014, 163) explains "jotería as a political project [that] can provide a matrix by which Chicana/o studies and related fields and movements can further decolonize themselves by making central the ways in which the politics of gender and sexuality are deeply imbricated in the analysis of race and movements of liberation." Like other revolutionary anti- and decolonizing efforts, the "political project of Jotería (and Joto/a identity) positions itself contrary to Euro-centered ideas of gender and sexuality" (Bañales, 157).

Two-spirited and jotería decolonization differs from queer, feminist, and white LGBTQ politics that "largely fail to underscore a relationship to power and colonization" (Bañales 157). Andrea Smith (2011, 48) puts it more directly, writing how queer theory "obfuscates the manner in which the 'queer' subject is also a settler subject." Further, queer Indigenous studies and jotería studies center "Indigenous [including Chican@] knowledge as a basis for social theory" (Driskill et al. 2011, 3). Pérez (2014, 143) adds that two-spirited/jotería studies provides an epistemology, a means of understanding colonialism, the tactics of colonial attacks on indigenous bodies, and who we are as indigenous people, based in "conceptions of knowledge that are articulated from a Jotería standpoint and that take into account the Jotería subject as an arbiter of knowledge."

GLBTQ2 and la jotería have further politicized the erotic for indigenous and Xican@ decolonial thought. The erotic "is a site of resistance and transformation for all Indigenous people" (Driskill et al. 2011, 16). Their insights build on Audre Lorde's "power of the erotic" and the numerous feminists of color who have theorized and utilized the erotic as a revolutionary site and weapon. The colonial strategy always involves taking the organic traditional power of the colonized/indigenous including the power of women in indigenous society and women's knowledge of the body and healing. Mujerista, indigenous feminist, and two-spirited/jotería scholars and activists locate the body and healing practices including reclamation of our foodways as a means of empowerment and decolonization (Calvo and Esquibel 2015).

Anarchist Politics Yearn for Freedom

Anarchist political theory and action influences many of the most important movements taking place in the period of late capitalism. These include such movements as Occupy, sectors of anti-globalization, permaculture, deep ecology and bioregionalism, queer, Zapatista solidarity, and food and environmental justice. As a self-identified indigenist anarchist I find anarchism a useful revolutionary political theory for anti-authoritarian, anti-colonial, alterNative praxis. While anarchism as theorized and practiced throughout history has contained a number of key flaws including its anti-nationalism, tendency to delve into a bourgeois individualism, hypermasculinity, insensitivity to issues of colonialism and racism, fetishizing of the working class, and industrialism, it promises the most flexibility, adaptability, and ability to correct its own flaws as well as the most consistent practice of anti-authoritarian theorizing and behavior. Throughout anarchist history women have corrected anarchist theory and praxis through writing and practicing anarchism from their unique position in the global colonial capitalist system. In addition, its ability to adapt to unique political, social, and economic conditions has allowed it, as a body of theory and practice, to incorporate different ideas, strategies, and people. Moreover, its basic outline aligns it well with indigenous American political and cultural organization. Anarchism adds to our anti-colonial, alterNative analysis a nearly two centuries-long critique of and active opposition to capitalism and the State.

Anarchism is a social movement and set of theories birthed along with capitalism in the 19th century. While anarchism has many different strands, most anarchists agree on a set of basic principles described below. Moreover, the version of anarchism I offer in the following aligns well with what has been called anarcho-communism. It differs only slightly from anarcho-syndicalism but is worlds apart from individualist anarchism and the more recent anarcho-capitalism; an oxymoron if there ever was one. While anarchist history has included individualists and debates rage over whether to include them in our movement, no anarchists I am aware of include anarcho-capitalists. Anarchists are against all forms of hierarchy. This has led us to see our primary enemies as the State and capitalism. Anarchists reject anarcho-capitalists and other so-called 'right-wing anarchists' who envision an anarchic (read: chaotic and without rules) world in which to make their riches. This is antithetical to the anarchist tradition and not what I intend when discussing anarchism.

Importantly, anarchism has always been a transnational movement. Anarchists and anarchism have developed through interaction with people in revolutionary struggle from across the globe. Michael Schmidt's *Cartography of Anarchism*, Jason Adams's "Non-Western Anarchisms: Rethinking the Global Context," and Maia Ramnath's *Decolonizing Anarchism* show the migrations of the international working classes and their interaction with one another leading to mutual understandings of capitalism and freedom. Anarchists' commitment to internationalism meant that anarchist ideas, strategies, and praxis developed in numerous centers of labor throughout the planet. Moreover, Jacqueline Lackey points to indigenous American roots of European anarchism. It is no wonder that traditional indigenous and anarchist rejection of private property and recognition of the inherent value of land mirror one another.

Anarchism seeks a world in which individuals have the most possible degree of freedom to develop one's abilities. Anarchists generally recognize that in order to reach our full potential we must be part of a social group. Small, decentralized community units based on participatory democracy and voluntary association serve as a model of societal organization common to many anarchists. We typically believe that this is the best organizational form for a society that seeks the most freedom, creativity, and happiness.

While anarchism has always been transnational and international the historiography of anarchism and practice of contemporary anarchists often falls short of its transnational anti-colonial potential. Many anarchists of color and anarchists from the Global South see a need to decolonize anarchism, which means to de-Europeanize. A respectful dialogue with indigenous anti-colonial theory and struggle and that of transnational feminism and two-spirited/jotería praxis can lead to this decolonization of anarchism while enriching each of the revolutionary perspectives and establishing new relationships.

Elements of an AlterNative Analysis

I use an anti-authoritarian, anti-colonial, alterNative analysis to examine Xican@ hip hop and street hop for its possibilities to decolonize the mind and open spaces for revolution. This alterNative analysis consists of elements from three revolutionary traditions: anarchism, indigenous decolonization, and transnational feminism. Each presents a common set of themes with varying emphases. As such, each praxis can add depth to the others. Together they form an integrated anti-authoritarian, anti-colonial, alterNative framework from which to consider pathways to an ecologically sound, non-hierarchical, free future.

I use insights from these traditions to establish an analytic framework with the following characteristics:

anti-capitalist	anti-State	anti-industrial	anti-hierarchical
anti-misogynist	place-based	participatory	decentralized
gender fluid	communal	inclusive of all our relations	

The next two chapters examine a selection of resistant Xican@ and street hop songs and images to assess the degree to which they contribute to anti-colonial aesthetics that aspires to the dismantling of oppressive ideologies and a renewal of indigenous worldview and identity.

Note

1 See ch. four, "Tejanas: Diasporic Subjectivities and Post-Revolutionary Identities," in Emma Perez's *Decolonial Imaginary: Writing Chicanas Into History* for the use of 'diaspora' as a useful concept to understand people of Mexican descent/Chican@s in the United States.

Bibliography

Adams, Jason. N.d. "Non-Western Anarchisms: Rethinking the Global Context." Downloaded from *The Anarchist Library*. www.theanarchistlibrary.org. November 2016.

Alfred, Taiaike. 2005. *Wasase: Indigenous Pathways of Action and Freedom*. Petersborough, ON: Broadview Press.

Alvarez, Luis. 2008. *The Power of the Zoot: Youth Culture and Resistance During World War II*. Berkeley: University of California Press.

Ball, Jared A. 2011. *I Mix What I Like: A Mixtape Manifesto*. Oakland, CA: AK Press.

Bañales, Xamuel. 2014. "Jotería: A Decolonizing Political Project." *Aztlán: A Journal of Chicano Studies*. 39:1: 155–165.

Calvo, Luz and Catriona Rueda Esquibel. 2015. *Decolonize Your Diet: Plant-Based Mexican-American Recipes for Health and Healing*. Vancouver: Arsenal Pulp Press.

Cervantes, Marco Antonio and Lilliana Patricia Saldaña. 2015. "Hip Hop and Nueva Cancion as Decolonial Pedagogies of Epistemic Justice." *Decolonization: Indigeneity, Education and Society*. 4:1.

Coulthard, G. S. 2014. *Red Skin, White Masks: Rejecting the Colonial Politics of Recognition*. Minneapolis: University of Minnesota Press.

Dhamon, Rita. 2015. "A Feminist Approach to Decolonizing Anti-Racism: Rethinking Transnationalism, Intersectionality and Settler Colonialism." *Feral Feminisms*. 4: 20–37.

Driskill, Qwo-Li, Chris Finley, Brian J. Gilley and Scott Lauria Morgensen (eds.). 2011. *Queer Indigenous Studies: Critical Interventions in Theory, Politics, and Literature*. Tucson: University of Arizona Press.

Editorial Collective. 2016. "Introduction." *Perspectives on Anarchist Theory*. 29.

Gaspar de Alba, Alicia. 1998. *Chicano Art Inside/Outside the Master's House: Cultural Politics and the CARA Exhibition*. University of Texas Press.

Gutiérrez, Ramon A. 1991. *When Jesus Came, the Corn Mothers Went Away: Marriage, Sexuality, and Power in New Mexico, 1500–1846*. Stanford: Stanford University Press.

Hall, Laura. 2016. "Indigenist Intersectionality: Decolonizing and Reweaving an Indigenous Eco-Queer Feminism and Anarchism." *Perspectives in Anarchist Theory*. 29: 81–94.

Hernandez, E. D. 2016. "Cultura Jotería: The Ins and Outs of Latina/o Popular Culture." In Aldama, F. L. (ed.). *The Routledge Companion to Latina/o Popular Culture*. New York: Routledge. Pp. 290–300.

Jaimes, M. Annette and Theresa Halsey. 1992. "American Indian Women: At the Center of Indigenous Resistance in North America." In M. Annette Jaimes (ed.). *State of Native America*. Cambridge, MA: South End Press. Pp. 31

Laskey, Jacqueline. 2011. "Indigenism, Anarchism, Feminism: An Emerging Framework for Exploring Post-Imperial Futures"." *Affinities Journal*. Special Edition on Anarch@Indigenism.

Lazar, Hillary. 2016. "Until All Are Free: Anarchism, Black Feminism, and Interlocking Oppression." *Perspectives in Anarchist Theory*. 29: 35–50.

Ngugi Wa Thiong'o. 1986. *Decolonising the Mind: The Politics of Language in African Literature*. Portsmouth, NH: Heinemann.

Peña, Devon G. 2014. "Revolutions Happen: Notes on the Crisis of Neoliberalism and the Subversiveness of the Common." April 18. Ejfood.blogspot.com.

Pérez, Daniel Enrique. 2014. "Jotería Epistemologies: Mapping a Research Agenda, Unearthing a Lost Heritage, and Building 'Queer Aztlán.'" *Aztlán: A Journal of Chicano Studies*. 39:1 (Spring): 143–154.

Perez, Emma. 1999. *The Decolonial Imaginary: Writing Chicanas into History*. Bloomington, IN: Indiana University Press.

Ramnath, Maia. 2011. *Decolonizing Anarchism*. Oakland, CA: AK Press.

Schmidt, Michael. 2013. *Cartography of Revolutionary Anarchism*. Oakland, CA: AK Press.

Simpson, Leanne B. 2014. "Land as Pedagogy: Nishnaabeg Intelligence and Rebellious Transformation." *Decolonization: Indigeneity, Education and Society*. 3:3: 1–25.

Smith, Andrea. 2011. "Queer Theory and Native Studies: The Heteronormativity of Settler Colonialism." In Driskill, Q., C. Finle, B. J. Gilley, and S. L. Morgensen (eds.). *Queer Indigenous Studies: Critical Interventions in Theory, Politics, and Literature*. Tucson: University of Arizona Press. Pp. 43–65.

3 New Millennial Maíz Narratives

Place and Identity in Xican@ Hip Hop

Anti-colonial, alterNative analyses link contemporary Xican@ expressions including hip hop to thousands of years of indigenous culture. Xican@ hip hop is a new millennial maíz narrative. In his analysis of "indigeneity and belonging in the Americas" Rodriguez (2015) traces a maíz narrative that can be seen, heard, and tasted throughout much of Abya Yala over the last 6,000 years. Centeotzintli (our sacred maíz) structured and continues to structure much of indigenous Mexican and Central American philosophy, religion, and social organization. Words and images from thousand-year-old stories reproduced by Rodriguez to today's Xican@ hip hop and the fight against transgenic pollution of Mexican corn crops exemplified by the "Sin Maíz, No Hay País" movement form an unbroken maíz narrative; an alterNative history of Xican@ people. This maíz narrative forcefully counters the colonizer's racial mythology and Manifest Destiny fantasies. It illustrates the indigeneity of people of Mexican descent and the common sense ecological, sustainable, and democratic practices that, if heeded, could save our planet from global burning and climate chaos (Wildcat 2009).

Chican@ poets and other writers during the Chicano Movement period often connected their Chican@ identity to place and indigeneity. Alurista, the most well-known and explicitly Xicano indigenous writer of the movement period, attempted to develop a decolonial mythology through his study of Mexican indigenous cultures and his published and performed poetry. His project complemented direct action by Chican@ activists by providing a new way of perceiving ourselves. Xican@ hip hop continues his project for a new generation using many of the same kinds of images and ideas. At the forefront of this project is place-claiming through ideas such as "Aztlán" and "la tierra." Maíz often stands in for place-based identity for Mexican@ and Xican@ artists, writers, and other cultural workers. Today members of the Chican@ Hip Hop Nation, Chican@ emcees, music producers, musicians, tattoo artists, muralists, danzantes, and graffiti writers attach their 21st-century Xican@ identities to maíz culture. Referring to maíz, they claim a right to this space called the United States, America, or North America since maíz has a 6,000-year history here. Xicano emcees, Los Nativos, exemplify this on their song "Sonido Indígena," rapping: "my lineage lives on/we represent the corn/from here to californ."

The following examination of a sample of Xican@ hip hop texts shows how Xican@ hip hop offers an alterNative analysis in service to the cause of decolonization. Jenell Navarro's (2015, 2) examination of indigenous hip hop provides an important starting point for understanding how the decolonial aesthetics of Xican@ hip hop open up the possibilities for anti-colonial action and new millennial indigenous identities through

> 1) disseminating a conscious pan-indigeneity through their lyricism and calls to alliance building; 2) retaining and teaching Indigenous languages through their songs, and 3) implementing a radical orality in their verses that revitalizes both Indigenous oral traditions/storytelling and the early politicized "message rap" of the 1970s and 1980s.

Maíz Narratives

The group, Kinto Sol, attach their identities to maíz when they claim that they are "hijos del maíz" and prominently display maíz in the clenched fist of Skribe (one of Kinto Sol's emcees) for the 2007 album, *Hijos del Maíz*. The song, "Hijos del Maíz" and its official video exemplify Xican@ hip hop connections to land and indigenous identity. The video opens in a milpa (cornfield) fading into a mural of a cornfield in front of which DJ Payback Garcia scratches on his turntables. Kinto Sol connect their urban Chicano existence of hip hop and concrete to the rural indigenous ideal of the milpa. The video, like hip hop generally, has multilayered meanings and images representing the Xican@ outlook in hip hop. Not only does Kinto Sol claim the right to be here through centeotzintli, but they claim urban spaces as Xican@ places using classic hip hop imagery including turntables and graffiti.

The next set of images in the video include short clips juxtaposing a Mexican man working la tierra and men in an office setting wearing suits. Kinto Sol explicitly connect themselves to the land via the images of the grandfatherly Mexicano working a milpa. The artists exalt Mexican/Xican@ tradition and mock the suit-wearing powerbrokers representing an Anglo, capitalist, colonialist tradition. The ridiculous men in suits wear hats with single words including avaricia (greed), ignorancia (ignorance), malinchismo (treachery), racismo (racism), and materialismo (materialism). The gluttonous powerbrokers eat a cake with a map of the United States and Mexico prominently decorating the top. They laugh boisterously, reveling in their destruction.

Indigeneity, land, and tradition are common themes in the video. The campesino is seen teaching a young boy the indigenous agricultural traditions of Mexican@s represented by the milpa. The cornfield stands in for Mexican@ traditional ecological knowledge (TEK) and practices. Kinto Sol asserts that this TEK needs to be passed down to new generations as an important part of the struggle against colonialism, capitalism, and racism. They further argue for a connection to a rapidly receding indigeneity amongst Mexican@s using the symbol of Benito Juarez to link their urban Xicanidad to indigenous Mexicanidad.

The lyrics to the song further provide clues to how Kinto Sol and Xican@ hip hop see themselves. They open the song rapping the following:

Mi abuelo murío trabajando la tierra	My grandfather died working the land
Nunca salío del monte siempre estuvo en la sierra	He never left the mountains he was always in the mountain range
Cuando yo era niño me regaló un azadón	When I was a boy he gave me a hoe.

The narrator's grandfather was a campesino who lived his life in the mountains and taught the narrator place-based ways represented by the gift of a hoe. As a campesino life was difficult and a cacique tried to strip him of the land. The narrator explains that even though the grandfather was courageous he ended up dying. The emcee poetically describes how death came to take away his grandfather's Tarascan soul. In the following lines Kinto Sol invoke their grandfather's indigenous Tarascan roots:

Aunque de coraje mi abuelo se muriera	Even though he was courageous, he died.
La muerte llegó y se tuvó que marchar	Death came and he had to march.
Su alma de Tarasco tuvó que volar	His Tarascan soul had to take flight.

Part of Xican@ identity and indigenous identity generally involves resistance to colonialism and racism (McFarland 2013). The 'warrior' is a common figure in Xican@/indigenous cultural politics. In the final lines of the first verse the narrator promises to avenge his grandfather's death using indigenous TEK. He declares:

te prometo que esas tierras yo las vuelvo a sembrar	I promise to return to sow those lands.
tu alma, mi tata, yo la tengo que vengar	Your soul, grandpa, I have to avenge
aunque el azadón por un rifle lo tenga que cambiar	even if I have to trade my hoe for a rifle.

The chorus further indicts the ruling classes as the chant "a los hijos de maíz/los han hecho sufrir/y los quieren ver morir." Power wants the 'children of corn' to suffer and see them die. The second verse follows up on this theme explaining that the hijos del maíz control nothing ("dueños de nada") and as a result suffer from hunger ("esclavos del hambre, miseria, violencia"), political neglect, and lack of employment, among other things. The emcee claims that all the politicians, no matter the party, care little for los hijos del maíz. Democracy doesn't exist in our current system according to Kinto Sol. Importantly, in this verse Kinto Sol critiques both the State and capitalism. The political parties are the playthings of the rich who make it easy for capital to exploit los hijos del maíz. They recognize that private property is key to the dispossession of indigenous and place-based people from their livelihoods and traditions.

Both indigenous and anarchist traditions reject private property. Since the 1840s anarchists have understood private property to be theft of the wealth of the Earth. Proudhon, the first self-proclaimed anarchist, argued against the capitalist notion of private property saying that "property is theft," allowing for one group of people to exploit other groups, and that "property is despotism," establishing authoritarian and oppressive relationships between owners and workers, peasants and tenants (McKay 2011, 6). Indigenous tradition establishes that humans are not entitled to the ownership of land and all our relations; that we are one of many relations in an ecosystem. Since the ownership of the means of production or private property is the key relationship under capitalist colonialism, both traditions' rejection of private property is a rejection of capitalism as a social and economic system.

Finally, Kinto Sol is not content to see themselves as indigenous victims of racist settler colonialism. The group of Xicanos invoke rebels Che Guevara and Pancho Villa as inspiration for their call to action. They call for Mexican@s/Xican@s (the sleeping giant) to rise up.

500 años escondida la verdad	500 years of hiding the truth
Cinco generaciones en la oscuridad	five generations in darkness
Llegó la luz. Terminó la tempestad	The light arrived. The storm ended.
El gigante dormido vuelve a despertar.	The sleeping giant is awakening.
El alma del che me aconseja.	Che's soul counsels me.
Villa me dice mochales la oreja	Villa tells me to cut off their ears.

They flesh out their understanding of their Xicano identity claiming that they are children of corn protecting the roots of their culture and destroying this corrupt system ("somos hijos del maíz protegiendo nuestra raiz eliminando el corrupto y cruel sistema"). They finish the song with Skribe in a shouting style explaining the spiritual battle in which they must engage.

cada uno de nosotros tenemos de terminar con el egoísmo	each of us has get rid of egoism
eliminando el yo y remplazarlo con el nosotros	eliminate it and replace it with 'us'
de la misma manera que nuestros antepasados coexistían	in the same way that our ancestors
colectivamente de una manera más espiritual	existed collectively in a more spiritual manner

Importantly, the spiritual battle is a collective battle. It must be fought in a collective manner similar to how their ancestors lived and to what many anarchists believe to be the ideal social organizational form. The song condemns materialismo, egoísmo, ignorancia, traición, and other energias negativas that have attacked indigenous people for 500 years. Oppression at the hands of racist colonizers must be overcome using TEK and other indigenous traditions. Kinto Sol claims that now is the time for a movement to reclaim their indigenous livelihood and dignity and repair the colonial damage ("es tiempo de reparar los daños a la raza de los cosmos").

Land, Place, and Language: An AlterNative Hip Hop Geography

The Xican@ experience is not an unadulterated pure indigeneity. The forces of colonialism, capitalism, and racism have forced Xican@ indigeneity to be a complex mix (mestizaje) of indigenous, urban, U.S., consumerist, Spanish, and Anglo European cultures. The city greatly influences the identities and experiences of urban new millennial Xican@s. For Xican@s in the Hip Hop Nation the city is place/homeland. Tolteka's album cover for his

Reflexiones en Yangna, Califaztlán (2008) illustrates the complex mestizaje of new millennial Xican@s. In the foreground the artist depicts an indigenous statue with a microphone emanating from the figure's head. In the background the artist renders the skyline of Yangna/Los Angeles. In a 2015 email Tolteka explained his place-claiming practices on his compact disc:

> On the *Reflexiones en Yangna Califaztlán* album, there are two words in the title itself that connect to three different conceptions of place names/ toponymy; one Eurocentric, two Indigenous-based. Califas, the xican@ calo repping of California, from Spaniard colonial times and the name of the state in dominant discourse today. The name, Aztlán, is rooted back in a pan-Nahua-Mexica indigeneity for the larger region (and mind state), and Yangna, out of respect for the Tongva, an original peoples of the Los Angeles area who named their settlement, Yangna (where la Plazita Olvera is now), long before any Europeans were present here.

As Tolteka points out, Spanish colonialism used place-claiming to erase indigenous presence. Their colonial power is illustrated in that the place names of the original peoples of today's United States Southwest, particularly California, have been lost to history. Tolteka and other Xican@ emcees make claims to la tierra of Califas, Yangna, etc. utilizing indigenous languages and place names.

Xican@ hip hop practitioners and enthusiasts symbolically reclaim space as lived place to which they have a right. Their assertion of indigeneity involves a political and economic argument in which 'to be Chicano and to live in Aztlán is to have historical precedence over Anglos in the Southwest; it is to declare a historical fact of descent' (Arteaga 1997, 9). Xican@ identity strikes at the heart of the colonial lie that would have us believe that Mexican@s/Xican@s are foreigners, illegals, criminals, and immigrants. Through an assertion of Xican@ identity, Xican@ emcees redraw the colonial map of North America offering an alternative hip hop cartography (Forman 2002). This mapping is a symbolic alterNative reterritorialization of indigenous homelands. Tolteka makes this alterNative cartography and indigenous identity explicit in the liner notes that accompany his compact disc. In the inside cover Tolteka reproduces the "Map of Disturnell" (used during the 'negotiations' leading to the Treaty of Guadalupe Hidalgo) to argue for our historical precedence in the Southwest. He explains why he reproduces the map:

> This is about acknowledging that we are native to the land currently found within the man made borders of this country. We are native to this continent, and we are not illegal aliens. . . . How can we be illegal

immigrants upon land which we've inhabited and had patterns of migration on since time immemorial?? [*sic*] The answer is that we can't be, and we won't be. We just have to awaken each other's consciousness up to this reality, acknowledging the fact that, as brown people, we are native to this land. We are indigenous people.

Navarro (2015, 8) explains that Tolteka's "'new' Indigenous historical geography [is] a way to contest settler expansionist formations of the U.S., and to challenge how such cartographies have been used as instruments of colonial domination." Tolteka's liner notes illustrate a pre-colonial past in which transnational interaction in trade and cooperation characterized Abya Yala. Instead of foreign invader, people of Mexican descent are original peoples with an ancient connection to the lands of Abya Yala. Our existence as indigenous who developed complex sustainable cultures over thousands of years shows that Chican@ urban problems result from theft of land, violence, and racism—the pillars of colonialism. Tolteka's indigenous historical geography contributes to native resurgence and anti-colonial praxis by presenting an indigenous history and deep connection to land.

The track "L@s Originales" illustrates Tolteka's and other Xican@ emcees' transnational indigeneity. The song uses a mix of indigenous flutes and hip hop drum patterns to create a driving beat to match his intensity. In the second verse he recognizes the numerous original peoples of North America using the hip hop rhetorical device of the 'shout-out' where an emcee names important people, places, and things. He shouts out the names of Mexican and Central American original peoples (Mexica, Maya, Huichol, Yaqui, Miskito), original peoples of Aztlán (Chumash, Cheyenne, Hopi), and the North American Plains (Lakota, Dakota). In the outro to the song his transnational indigenous identity includes resistance to colonialism. Here his shout-out to the original peoples takes a militant turn. Tolteka announces a transnational list of names of indigenous and Chican@ decolonial and anti-racist warriors including Cuauhtemoc, Tupac Amaru, Tecumseh, Tiburcio Vasquez, Pacal, Ricardo Flores Magón, Adelita, Emiliano Zapata, Frida Kahlo, Comandante Ramona, Corky Gonzalez, Bert Corona, and Anna Mae Aquash. Emphasizing the resistant act, Tolteka uses a chorus of voices to shout "que viva!" or "presente!" after each name in the style of Chican@ and Latin@ radical organizations. The chorus of "que viva!" and "presente!" by participants in radical cultural and political activities connects them to a lineage of resistance that is present and alive in current struggles. The radical spirits of our predecessors are invoked to strengthen the resolve of contemporary anti-colonial, anti-racist warriors.

Tolteka makes explicit many of the values and the place-based epistemological and ontological foundations of his indigenous identity in the liner notes to his compact disc. The notes, written in Spanish, which he calls "our other language of colonization," explain indigenous tradition:

> En la tradición nativa humildad, dignidad y respeto mutuo son la escencia. Pensar que eres mejor o peor que otra persona, no tiene lugar en esta tradición. Hay que dar el mismo respeto que queremos recibir. . . . El balance es la clave. El balance es lo que busco diario apasionamente. L@s que quieran juzgarme, juzquenme. L@s que quieran construir, vamos construyendo en este movimiento de tiempo eterno.
>
> [In the native tradition humility, dignity and mutual respect are the essence. To think that you are better or worse than another person has no place in this tradition. You have to give the same respect that you want to receive. . . . Balance is the key. Balance is what you passionately seek daily. Those who want to judge me, judge me. Those who want to construct, let's construct this movement of eternal time.]

Tolteka's dignity, mutual respect, humility, respect for life, and balance reflect the indigenous values of Abya Yala. Place-based peoples typically base their societies on these values because having been in their place for millennia they observe that interdependence is a law of the universe, diversity is required of any functional eco- or social system, and that life exists in a delicate balance that is easily disrupted by prideful or greedy humans. This biocentric, land-based ethic is reflected in dichos (sayings) including in lak 'ech (Lacandon Mayan for "You are my other me") and mitakuye oyasin (Lakota for "all our relations"). Inherent in land-based ethics is a critique of capitalism, private property, capitalist consumer values, and colonialism. Indigenous Mexican@s learn as children not to be sin verguenzas (someone without shame); to respect other's right to exist and thrive; to be generous; to take only what you need.

The spiritual values expressed by land-based people reflect the abovementioned ethics. We included a sense of equity and respect for women, men, and two-spirited people. The origin stories of indigenous people reflect the importance of women and religious belief systems often center women deities or a Pachamama (Mother Earth)-type figure. In "Decimas" Tolteka examines this aspect of native tradition, rapping that "la Virgen de Guadalupe sagrada es la Tonantzin" (the sacred Virgin of Guadalupe is Tonantzin). In his email communication he explains how he connects indigenous spirituality including understandings of gender with contemporary Xican@ identity and resistance to European-imposed spiritual tradition:

> The first verse is relevant because it connects the deeply respected la Virgen de Guadalupe in Mexico, and connects her to Tonantzin, the

mother earth connection the indigenous of Mexico had before colonial Catholicism replaced her with La Virgen; the second verse in Nahuatl is relevant, because it hits up the region and continent I'm representing in Nahuatl, Aztlanahuak and Ixachilan, and also gives thanks to the four directions; and the third verse is relevant too, mainly because of the lyrics "tenemos el maíz en la raíz, la sangre, la cultura, y la memoria genetica, poetica, autentica."

Indigenous spiritualities strive for balance and respect and recognize our interdependence with each other and all our relations. That the Earth is viewed as Mother-female in indigenous systems is not anthropomorphizing and/or gender stereotyping but recognition of the similarities that it has with human and other-than-human beings. The Earth, like women, creates life. Thus, it is to be revered. It is not to be dominated as in the European Judeo-Christian religions in which women are equated with a nature that is to be dominated by male humans.[1] Because indigenous religious systems are based on land ethics including and especially balance, respect, and interdependence, they include a wide variety of deities, both women, men, and other. Some look toward these differing religious systems as the fundamental source of difference between Europeans and indigenous people. The human as superior/man as superior perspective is foundational to the greed and violence at the heart of capitalist colonialism. As such, any anti-colonial alterNative praxis incorporates land-based ethics.

Finally, Tolteka and other Xican@ emcees use the indigenous language of Nahuatl. Tolteka uses Nahuatl on several tracks while other emcees only use phrases or concepts from Nahuatl. That they use Nahuatl to situate themselves in an alterNative geography is significant. Since "language holds knowledge, history and culture" (Zepeda 2014, 130) it does important anti-colonial work by 'decolonizing the mind' and reintroducing indigenous concepts necessary for understanding and embodying 21st-century Xican@ indigeneity. Susy J. Zepeda explains the importance of language use to decolonizing projects in her analysis of the sculpture work of Gina Aparicio. "The exposure of this language to her (mostly urban and 'detribalized') audiences provides a consciousness of Indigenous concepts not available if Chicanas/os and Latina/os are only engaging with the Spanish and English languages" (Zepeda, 131). The ancient words spoken in Nahuatl hold ideas, power, ways of being and seeing that the conquerors' languages cannot properly convey. Thus, if decolonization requires epistemic decolonization, then the work of Xican@ and other native musicians, artists, and writers is essential to the revolutionary process.

Urban Xican@ Hip Hop Anti-colonialism: Anarchism and Indigeneity

Veteran emcee and Xicano warrior Olmeca has a long history of cultural production celebrating people of Mexican descent as indigenous people and claiming an indigenous identity characterized by human-land relations, resistance to colonialism, and land-based epistemology and ontology. The lyrics, music, and video to his "Por El Suelo" (2013) from the *Brown is Beautiful* compact disc epitomizes urban Xicanidad as expressed in hip hop. The song begins with Tarahumara dancers from the Tinkus Wapurys tradition in full performance dress dancing to heavy hip hop bass drums, handclaps, a steady rapid high hat, and the repetition of Toto La Momposina singing "por el suelo."[2] When Olmeca begins rapping the lyrics "Como Tarahumara firmly grounded and I travel slow" he appears in front of the dancers who remain the central visual reference throughout the song. Olmeca next raps:

> Live, life, every step I take I grow/on the ground is where it happens that where people go/Por el suelo./Follow steps of the great, Nina Simone!/Si vivo en las nubes, no vivo. Y por eso/por el suelo camina el pueblo. Todos igual como grano de arena.

Interspersed with Olmeca and the Tarahumara danzantes are b-boys spinning on the ground 'where it happens', Nina Simone performing, and images of Brown Berets marching and "Brown is Beautiful" signs from the Chicano Movement era. Olmeca's indigenous Mexicanidad is one of humble dignity where all are equal like a grain of sand ("como grano de arena"). Since to live one's life in the clouds is not living ("si vivo en las nubes, no vivo") it is important to stay connected to the material realities of earth. For this reason, the Earth is the people's path ("y por eso, por el suelo camina el pueblo"). Olmeca's indigenous epistemology includes attention to nature, humility, interconnectedness, dignity, and equality. Throughout the song and video, images of traditional danzante troupe members and marching militants from the Brown Berets move in sync with the ferocious beat provided by high hats and handclaps and Olmeca's expressive and percussive voice and rapid-fire delivery. Olmeca's indigeneity foregrounds difference, tradition, and polyculturality. Images and lyrics refer to a wide range of influences on urban indigeneity. Stokely Carmichael, the Black Panther Party, Mercedes Sosa, a woman Zapatista comandante, Fela Kuti, Richie Valens, and Nina Simone appear together as the material of Olmeca's transnational self-claiming.

With "Corn Grenade Renegade" (2010) Olmeca further epitomizes the 21st-century anti-colonial urban Xican@. From a working-class perspective, he ties militant resistance to 'cultura' and maíz. The boom-boom-bap beat, polyrhythms, and prominent blues guitar place Xican@ identity within an urban African diasporan-infused and polycultural environment. Olmeca raps:

> What's the weapon of your choice?/Truth and cultura./Bombing corn grenades/I'm a full blown renegade./This administration still follows a chain./War is still the answer./What's the meaning of change?/Business as usual. Is that the meaning of change?/Homeland Security, a tactic against the poor.

Olmeca's anti-colonial aesthetics offer a militant urban Xicanism@ and a critique of the State through the allusions to President Obama, whose candidacy as a viable presidential candidate in 2008 relied on the idea of 'change' and the naming of the Department of Homeland Security. His role as cultural worker in the anti-colonial struggle involves 'bombing the truth before I let them take me away'. His "bombing" refers to the hip hop practice of putting one's name or concept out for mass public consumption, e.g., putting up hundreds of graffiti tags. He wants to get his truth out to as many people as often as he can before he suffers the fate of most revolutionaries: prison, exile, or death.

Ultimately, Olmeca presents a political subjectivity akin to Alfred's indigenous anarchism. On the songs "Anarquia" from the *Sons of Anarchy* television show soundtrack and "Zapatistas Live" (2012), he offers two sides of an anarchist coin; militant resistance and a well-ordered egalitarian society. On "Anarquia" Olmeca provides a militant black bloc-like anarchist perspective rapping over heavy metal guitars:

Instituciones legales es el desorden	[Legal institutions are the disorder.
Tan obvio que casi no hay necesidad que les informen	It is so obvious that I don't need to tell you.
la norma de la sociedad es fría	The societal norm is cold
Vía de la anarquía mía es el orden	The anarchist way is my order.]
Guerrillero soy	[I am a guerrilla.
hacia al frente voy	to the front I go
solo no estoy	I am not alone.
la guerra empieza hoy	The war starts today.]
Habré los ojos a la realidad.	[Open your eyes to reality.
Habré la boca pa' pedir piedad	Open your mouth to ask for piety.

Camina lentamente a la vecindad	Walk slowly through the neighborhood
Siente la marea siente marea	Feel the sickness, feel the sickness
De la desigualdad en la ciudad.	Of inequality in the city.]
Cuidado te digo yo soy bendecido	[When I tell you that I am blessed
por ancianos que lo han vivido	by the ancestors that have lived
mi camino no es fingido	my path is not fixed.]

The call for a direct engagement with the legal institutions of the 'cold' societal disorder mirrors the perspective of revolutionary anarchists who believe it necessary to engage in direct action and armed struggle with oppressive forces. He implores listeners to open their eyes to urban social problems. Ultimately, he calls for people to join the revolutionary way of his ancestors; a way that we might call anarcho-indigenist.

Olmeca addresses what such a way might look like in his "Zapatistas Live!" The song emphasizes autonomy as the key revolutionary strategy and practice in a free society. Over a beat sustained by African hand drums, Olmeca details his understanding of Zapatista history and theory of revolutionary autonomy. Among the lyrics are the following:

> They didn't take state power or seize control. They didn't realize a new constitution . . . I saw them toil through the rain, thunderstorm, and sun that boiled. No media, no gatherings, no nonsense. Just exercising their right to be free. Government programs surrounding liberated territory. Government building empty structures next to the Zapatistas building autonomy. Tourist attractions next to cultural projects. One selling culture and the other rescuing it from capitalist exposure. . . . The enemy knows the Zapatistas are real and so are their tactics. For more dangerous to a government isn't armed conflict but knowing that they can be obsolete. Obsolete because an entire people created their own good government, schools and clinics, their own collectives and in the process came to fully grasp that the only solution to living in dignity is to build it yourself.

The Zapatista strategy of autonomy might be seen as a model of indigenous anarchism. Their focus has been to disengage from capitalist colonialism by reinstalling indigenous practices in governance and social organization, using traditional ecological knowledge; redefining themselves through stories, music, and ritual; and insisting on local direct action for self-determination while understanding the importance of transnational solidarity and exchange. Instead of a liberal politics of protest involving negotiations and reform of the capitalist settler-colonial governments, they forged an anti-colonial, anti-authoritarian indigenous self-determination. Olmeca also references the Zapatistas and their attention to revolutionary dignidad in his overall body of work. This indigenous means of relating and understanding of oneself in relation to a community offers an indigenous replacement for the greed and violence of capitalist colonialism (Subcomandante Marcos 2002).

Diosas Guerrerillas

As in most areas of Hip Hop, men predominate in Xican@ hip hop. Thus, it is inevitable that the anti-colonial texts produced therein will be from the standpoint of men. Xican@ hip hop texts of the reclamation of Indigenous identity and its redefinition for the new millennium skew towards masculinity. Though European-style patriarchy influences Xicano men, Indigenous understandings of gender temper their masculine worldview. Xicano emcees also discuss women's issues, women's power, and women's spirituality. Tolteka's song "Decimas" is a good example. But, it is the Xicana emcees such as Rain Flowa and Cihuatl Ce who offer a Xicana indigenous, transnational perspective. Additionally, Xicanas in hip hop and activist circles put a check on patriarchal tendencies and provide a complex picture of Xican@ life and struggle. While few in number, Xicana emcees alert us to the triple oppression they face in society and in hip hop. Asserting a "feminine place of power" they "produce presence, recognize the place where one is from, and celebrate it by articulating the struggle for the right to be there" (Peláez Rodríguez 2016, 191). Xicana emcees, like many feminists of color, seek to 'decolonize their bodies' through revolutionary ritual performance that emphasizes place and feminine spirituality. They associate themselves with and invoke Coatlicue or Diosa Madre (Mother Goddess). Their feminine reclamation of their indigenous identities offer healing from the traumas of colonialism (Peláez Rodríguez 2016, 197). Their rituals of reclamation including rap rituals link their 21st-century United States urban indigeneity to ancient ancestral knowledge and worldview from a Xicana perspective.

I have been following Rain Flowa (pka Kiawitl Xochitl) since the early 2000s when Lady Binx, as she was then known, was one of a trio of emcees comprising the group Almas Intocables (McFarland 2008). In her career and community life/work she has demonstrated a consistent commitment to developing and communicating an indigenous consciousness and lifestyle. As a danzante (traditional Mexica dancer) and emcee, Rain Flowa performs a Xicana consciousness invoking the cosmos and the land while seeking guidance from indigenous ancestors and their traditions. "Cosmic Buttafly" contributes to the redefinition and resurgence of indigenous identity connecting ancestral tradition to land and the cosmos. The music fuses indigenous Mesoamerican sounds, rhythms, and instruments including rattles, drums, and flutes with African diasporan rhythms. Over the mesmerizing musical foundation Rain Flowa raps melodically:

> Ancient truth never faded./Once you're in line movements align/Portals open up. Spirit's divine/are waiting./We all have a dream to share./ Unblock your heart become aware./Cosmic knowledge is everywhere. Such a precious gift that never can compare/to what we think and feel./ Energy must move in a positive field./Put yourself freely along the wind.

Rain Flowa's indigeneity is informed by 21st-century urban placemaking. A live performance video of the song "Indigenous Side" (2011) shows Kiawitl (Rain Flowa) accompanied by a DJ, a drum machine, and a vocal backing track. Kiawitl's physicality and rapping style along with the hip hop music and instrumentation point to an urban polycultural influence while her lyrics locate her within indigenous tradition. She, like all Xican@ hip hop performers, uses language of resistance to settler colonialism and white supremacy and offers indigenous resurgence as the basis of a new indigenous way of life. In the first verse she raps:

> Got the bass bumpin from the trunks./It parallels our war drums./Gettin ready for defense of our little ones./Within this homeland our security's been breached/and this invasion runs five centuries deep./When you gonna recognize who you are inside?/You better hurry up before we run outta time.

Similar to how indigenous ancestors may have used war drums, today's urban indigenous use 'bass': the hip hop characteristic of listening to music loudly with heavy emphasis on bass instruments. Hip hop gets them ready to defend their children, their land, and culture from 500 years of colonialism. Part of the necessary work to develop people into warriors is to help them define themselves without reference to the colonizer's definitions. In order to fight for freedom, people must believe that they are worthy of freedom, which in a racially stratified society means ethnic pride. Or as Kiawitl says in the chorus of the song: "refining the pride in our indigenous side./ Yes, we're finding the pride in our indigenous side."

Perhaps more importantly than the lyrical reclamation of indigeneity, indigenous dignity, and indigenous pride, Rain Flowa embodies native resurgence through her performance. Today, Kiawitl focuses her creative energies on danza Azteca and indigenous song and dance. But, even in her hip hop performances she displays her indigenous side. Videos show Rain Flowa performing with Yetlanezi, a group that performs electro-indigenous music. The trio of musicians from Guadalajara describe their music as "a mixture of textures that blends ancient indigenous earth-based instruments with the electronic influences of the digital age" (Yetlanezi 2017). In performances with Yetlanezi, Rain Flowa ad libs and uses her voice as a percussion instrument adding to the reverently played, densely layered indigenous rhythms. DJ Trajik Sol adds another layer of hip hop on this incredible performance with his electronic musical additions. Kiawitl's improvised vocal performance exemplifies the polycultural nature of 21st-century urban U.S. Xican@ experience. Her dress alone points to the syncretism of today's Xicanisma. She wears a white t-shirt with a small picture and lettering, blue jeans, and a black bucket hat (all common fashion in the hip hop nation), an indigenous woven bag often found in Southern Mexico and Central America and coral and turquois necklaces common amongst the Pueblos and other peoples in New Mexico and other parts of Aztlán. Her rap and blues-style singing bear witness to the African diasporan aspects of this polycultural indigenous anti-colonial praxis. Finally, her lyrics put a fine point on this rap ritual, as she repeatedly chants, 'we're all indigenous' over a mesmerizing rhythmic crescendo.

Rain Flowa's presence and success in independent hip hop offers a challenge to the misogynist lie that hip hop and cultural representation are the purview of men. A macho male nationalism undergirds much of hip hop, cultural nationalist, and indigenous resistance politics. Rain Flowa's virtuosity and the breadth of her creativity speak to the importance of women in the arts and anti-colonial politics. She presents the image of a Xicana warrior in her lyrics and embodies this in her activism and community arts work. She insists that we reclaim our 'indigenous side' that includes a complex gender politics in which women have played distinct yet necessary roles. She traces her understanding of herself as an indigenous Xicana through religious understanding and often refers to indigenous female gods Tonantzin, Coatlicue, and la Virgen de Guadalupe.

Overall, her gender politics seems to rely on heteronormativity. It does not speak to the gender fluidity necessary for an anti-authoritarian, anti-colonial, alterNative political practice and indigenous-based social organization. A truly anti-authoritarian and free society would eliminate biases such as heteronormativity and the homophobia and transphobia that follow from its logic and practice. An anti-colonial society would reject the Euro-Christian gender and sexuality classification systems and prejudices and practice indigenous gender flexibility and permeable gender boundaries. Moreover, an indigenous society would replace the logic of the colonial gender/sex system with the gender fluid and complex systems of most indigenous groups. In addition, two-spirited and jotería perspective and experience under colonialism and capitalism offer a much more complete and nuanced analysis of the problems we face.

Conclusion

Xican@ hip hop including Tolteka, Kinto Sol, Olmeca, El Vuh, Jehuniko, Rain Flowa, Los Nativos, and Aztlán Underground uses music, lyrics, and artwork to claim an indigenous identity, reterritorialize the spaces we inhabit, make political statements, and teach young people a Xican@ indigenous perspective. Tolteka, for example, presents Xican@ indigeneity as based in traditions of mutual respect, humility, and dignity. He wants people to 'wake up' and have a shift in consciousness. Kinto Sol makes a similar point emphasizing indigenous connection to place and the collective nature of indigenous society. And Xicana emcees open our ears to the belief that an anti-authoritarian, anti-colonial, alterNative praxis, or "true revolution[,] has no room for male bravado and sexism" (Rodriguez 2008, 145).

The cultural work of these artists and activists is an essential part of native resurgence. It serves as decolonial pedagogical praxis (Cervantes and Saldaña 2015) as organic indigenous pedagogues steeped in native tradition and engaged in a process of re-indigenization teach the Indigenous Knowledge of their ancestors to new generations through the transnational sights, sounds, and sensations of hip hop. They contribute to the thousands-years-old maíz narratives of Mesoamerica and to a project of revolutionary dignity as theorized and practiced by the Zapatistas. They are, as Jenell Navarro (2015, 3) presciently explains,

> revolutionary cultural texts . . . the hip-hop produced by politically conscious Indigenous artists . . . aid in the processual work of decolonization by reinforcing this collective pan-Indigenous consciousness that forms the foundation of transnational movements for Indigenous rights in the Americas.

Zepeda adds that hip hop is transnational and diasporic as "it defies the boundaries of the nation-state." Xican@ emcees lay claim to place and the right to exist as humans and as Xican@ indígenas wherever they choose regardless of colonial State boundaries. They see history and geography from an anti-colonial alterNative perspective and connect themselves to indígenas of the Mesoamerican Diaspora as well as indigenous peoples across the Americas and internationally. Their numerous references to and 'shout-outs' to indigenous nations, groups, communities, and individuals and their claims to intimate connection to people, events, and ideas of different indigenous groups illustrate the transnational and diasporic aspects of Xican@ hip hop indigeneity.

While Xican@ hip hop reflects an anti-authoritarian, anti-colonial alter-Native analysis, its underdeveloped gender analysis and little room for la jotería limits its liberatory potential. Dialogue with other Xican@/indigenous traditions including muxerista, gay Chicano, la jotería, and two-spirited would serve the Xican@ anti-colonial analysis in hip hop.

Notes

1 The Judeo-Christian tradition has interpreted "God's" instruction to Adam as having dominion over both nature and women. This interpretation of "God's" directions to Adam has been challenged by a new 'Black Environmental Liberation Theology' (Glave 1990) and by conservationist Wendell Berry (1990), who argues that "God's" directions to Adam in Genesis made him a steward and caretaker of the Earth and not a conqueror.
2 See Olmeca's website olmeca.bandcamp.com for details concerning the making of his music.

Bibliography

Arteaga, Alfred. 1997. *Chicano Poetics: Heterotexts and Hybridities*. Cambridge: Cambridge University Press.

Berry, Wendell. 1990. *What Are People For? Essays*. Berkeley, CA: Counterpoint.

Cervantes, Marco Antonio and Lilliana Patricia Saldaña. 2015. "Hip Hop and Nueva Cancion as Decolonial Pedagogies of Epistemic Justice." *Decolonization: Indigeneity, Education and Society*. 4:1.

Forman, Murray. 2002. *The Hood Comes First: Race, Space and Place in Rap and Hip Hop*. Middletown, CT: Wesleyan University Press.

Glave, Diane D. 1990. "Black Environmental Liberation Theology." In Glave, D. D. and M. Stoll (eds.). *'To Love the Wind and the Rain': African Americans and Environmental History*. University of Pittsburgh Press. Pp. 189–199.

McFarland, Pancho. 2013. *The Chican@ Hip Hop Nation: Politics of a New Millennial Mestizaje*. East Lansing: Michigan State University Press.

———. 2008. *Chicano Rap: Gender and Violence in the Postindustrial Barrio*. Austin: University of Texas Press.

McKay, Iain. 2011. "Introduction: General Idea of the Revolution in the 21st Century." In Iain McKay (ed.), *Property Is Theft! A Pierre-Joseph Proudhon Anthology*. Oakland, CA: AK Press. Pp. 1–52.

Navarro, Jenell. 2015. "Word: Hip-Hop, Language, and Indigeneity in the Americas." *Critical Sociology*. Pp. 1–15.

Olmeca. olmeca.bandcamp.com.

Peláez Rodríguez, Diana C. 2016. "Chicana Hip Hop: Expanding Knowledge in the L.A. Barrio." In Castillo-Garsow, Melissa and Jason Nichols (eds.). *La Verdad: An International Dialogue on Hip Hop Latinidades*. Columbus: Ohio State University Press. Pp. 183–202.

Rodriguez, Lori Beth. 2008. "Mapping Tejana Epistemologies: Contemporary (Re) Constructions of Tejana Identity in Literature, Film and Popular Culture." PhD dissertation. University of Texas at San Antonio.

Rodriguez, Robert C. 2015. *Our Sacred Maíz Is Our Mother: Indigeneity and Belonging in the Americas.* Tucson: University of Arizona Press.

Subcommandante Marcos. 2002. *Our Word Is Our Weapon: Selected Writings.* New York: Seven Stories Press.

Tolteka. 2015. Personal correspondence via email. August 4.

———. 2008. *Reflexiones en Yangna, Califaztlan.* Compact disc.

Wildcat, Daniel. 2009. *Red Alert: Saving the Planet with Indigenous Knowledge.* London: Fulcrum.

Yetlanezi. 2017. "Facebook page." www.facebook.com/pg/Yetlanezi-20500308951 1034/about/?ref=page_internal

Zepeda, Suzy J. 2014. "Queer Xicana Indígena Cultural Production: Remembering Through Oral and Visual Storytelling." *Decolonization: Indigeneity, Education & Society.* 3:1: 119–141.

4 Place in the New Pinto Poetics

Chican@ Street Hop's Anti-authoritarianism

Since colonization the settler-colonial prison and 'justice' systems have shaped the experience and cultural expression of many Chican@s (Mirandé 1987; Paredes 1958). The pinto poet of the Chicano movement and post-movement period reflects the colonized status of people of Mexican descent in the United States. The places of residence and communities of Chican@s are controlled by others particularly landlords, employers, and governments. Moreover, treated like foreigners, we are often displaced and forced to migrate (Villa 2000). Given the influence of displacement and lack of control of our spaces it is no wonder that place-claiming and place-making figure prominently in Chican@ cultural expression, including that of the pinto poet and Chican@ street hop (Olguín 2010; Villa 2000).

Streets, Prisons, and Urban Chicanidad

The pinto is an outlaw figure. He is often a social bandit; one who breaks illegitimate colonial laws and is accepted, even exalted, by his community. The revolutionary Chicano tradition celebrates the outlaw/social bandit. The influence of anarchist Ricardo Flores Magón on Chican@ revolutionary thought includes his writings on the illegitimacy of capitalist law and the necessity of the "outlaw" for emancipation. In his "Outlaws" (2005 (1910), 241–242) he explains:

> The true revolutionary is an outlaw par excellence. The man who adjusts his actions to conform to the law, can be, a good domestic animal, but not a revolutionary. The law conserves; the revolution renews. For the same reason, if one must renew, one must begin by breaking the law. Claiming that the revolution can be made within the law is lunacy, is a contradiction. The law is a yoke, and he who wants to free himself from the yoke must break it . . . Expropriation is achieved through trampling over the law, not by lifting it to the heavens. For this reason, revolutionaries must necessarily be outlaws.

The pinto poet tradition exemplified by Ricardo Sanchez, Jimmy Santiago Baca, and Raul Salinas critiques the State, capitalism, racism, and colonialism. Importantly, they illustrate "the multiform creative practices by which Chicanos have attempted to materially reconstitute and expressively represent places of community well-being against the degradations to which those places have been subject" (Villa 2000, 157). In the pinto tradition as in street hop, places of marginality, dispossession, and violence such as prisons and inner-city streets in the era of the War on Drugs have a profound effect on identity. Olguín (2010) shows how pinto identity develops in part through resistance to Chicano prisoners' degrading experiences in the prison and mass incarceration systems. Like Xican@ identity, pinto identity is a resistant identity (not without its contradictions as Olguín points out in his study) and pinto poets exemplify this in their work as they "interrogate the circumstances and sources of their subaltern life in the free world, as well as their liminal and transformative experiences in prison" (2010, 71). The inner-city barrios create a new pint@ identity for contemporary Chican@ youth. Their subaltern status especially as demonstrated in their interactions with the carceral state and their resistance to it lead some to a "sick," "psycho," or "loco" identity (McFarland 2013, 36–40). Chican@ street hop emcees, like pinto poets, express their sick/psycho/loc@ identities in their song titles, lyrics, tattoos, and other art.[1] Through their art these street hop emcees reflect and develop a loco episteme rooted in their constant attempts to defy "the system." This rebel and transgressive spirit connects street hop culture to that described by the 1960s- and 1970s-era pinto poetry and the older traditions of the outlaw, social bandit, and indigenous resistance.

In pinto and street hop traditions we find both bravado and vulnerability. Lines such as this from Ricardo Sanchez point to the violence of barrioization and the prison system and the toll they take on Chicanos: "He tried vainly and then cried tears upon tears upon the steel prison tiers" ("Tiers/Tears"). The emotional toll that the legal system took on Sanchez and other Chicano pintos has continued and expanded with the War on Drugs and mass incarceration. Lyrics by Chicano street hop emcees connect them to the pinto poetry tradition and update it for the new millennium. Thief Sicario's "Tearz of Rage" mirrors Sanchez's "Tiers/Tears" in which he explains why he writes, stating, "upon the page my soul I vomit." Like Sanchez the prison for Thief offers tears of pain and writing down his experiences provides catharsis. In the chorus he explains the emotions evoked by the prison system:

Tears of rage/break it down like a gauge [shotgun]/take it down on the page/and make a sound out my rage./Hate the sounds of a cage./Through the cell I'm stompin./Prison's the graveyard/my cell, the coffin.

The mass incarceration system has not only made prison a horrendous place for many Chican@s but the marginalized barrios in which many working-class Chican@s live often confront them as dangerous. Juan Zarate offers important examples of this in his song "Santuario." Zarate depicts his Chicago barrio as a place of ignorance and violence *and* as his sanctuary. While the barrio contains innumerable dangers it is also home where Chicanit@s find love and acceptance. Zarate's song suggests that reterritorialization and place-making in Chican@ barrios finds possibility in the love and acceptance that many find there. He remarks at the beginning of his song that "a veces es lo peor, cabrón, pero aqui nos acepta" (sometimes it's the worst, man, but here we are accepted). Revolutionary love and dignity form an integral part of a progressive Chican@ street hop identity without which the loco episteme can turn towards the homophobic, misogynist, racist, and oppressive that haunt colonized people's attempts to change their subaltern status.[2] As discussed earlier, colonizers use racist misogyny as a means of war against native populations. All the better for the colonizer if they can get colonized men to attack native women, further driving a wedge between Indigenous people.

The 'street' or 'calle' is the most common ground for the contestation of space found in Chican@ street hop and the loco episteme. Images of the street and encounters with the criminal justice system form the bulk of the foundation upon which street hop emcees tell their tales of life on the 'sickside'. The sickside is a place that many street hop emcees and urban Chican@ youth create or imagine out of the colonial conditions of the inner city. Some urban working-class Chican@ youth respond to barrioization/colonization through reterritorializing (or remaking) streets creating the sickside. The realities of mass incarceration and a 300-year long history of state repression and violence told in Chican@ hip hop narratives reveal the colonized status of Xican@s. Chican@ emcees discuss the State's social and physical control of space. The War on Drugs shapes the experience of many working-class Chican@s. Images and discussions of drugs, guns, gangs, and police in street hop texts illustrate and critique this aspect of repression.

Psycho Realm, more than most Chican@ hip hop groups, articulates the critique of State containment (barrioization) and their attempts to survive and thrive amongst the neglect and violence. Their song "Palace of Exile" from *A War Story: Book II* (2003) explicitly connects the War on Drugs and mass incarceration to capitalist economic imperatives. Speaking to young Chicanos (the "#1 Target" of the mass incarceration system according to a song of the same name) they warn that "no matter what your record is or how many you've killed/you could be clean as a whistle homey but still/the palace (prison) was built for you." Psycho Realm adds first-person accounts to what Michelle Alexander (2012, 87) describes in her work. Due to practices of overcharging, many innocent young men plea bargain in order to take a lesser sentence out of fear of being found guilty of a more serious crime. In the current climate, Chicanos/Mexicanos are assumed to be guilty. Drug sweeps, immigration raids, surveillance technology, mass media, and drug enforcement funding label urban Chicanos as criminals. In addition, poverty and racism create barrio conditions in which even those who are "clean as a whistle" wear a stigma of deviance and are prime candidates for the palaces that Psycho Realm describes. They rap:

> Flood the streets with cannabis/crystal meth handle this/get you fucked up/then serve you guns with high calibers/give you ghetto fame every time you act crazy/knuckleheads bringing heat to 'hoods daily/got cops ready to serve you just waiting/to take you to the palace . . . if in jail get petty money for labor skills/while stock holders sell and make money off shit you build.

Psycho Realm offers an organic street intellectual perspective on mass incarceration, techniques of barrioization, and chemical warfare meted out against working-class Chican@s. Like Alexander (2012), Parenti (2000), Davis (2003), Villa (2000) and others, Psycho Realm shows how capitalist colonialism uses racism and incarceration to control populations and exploit resources. Mass incarceration is big business as brown bodies become commodities like during slavery in the United States or the murder of natives for the price of their scalps (Dunbar-Ortiz 2015, 65), and as the labor of these same commodified bodies is exploited. Today Psycho Realm sees parallels with a history of colonial uses of biological and chemical warfare on previous generations of indigenous people in the forms of disease, starvation, and alcohol. Dangerous street drugs like 'crystal meth' destroy brown bodies while police clash with illicit entrepreneurs (a new comprador class) who do the colonizer's bidding by poisoning Chican@ communities.

However, Chicano hip hop narratives symbolically reterritorialize their colonized urban places. The "street" determines the urban ecology of contemporary working-class youth of color and occupies a prominent place in their narratives. Here, in the street, young Chican@s have experiences that influence their development. Here, in the street, barrioized Chican@s interact with the police and migra but also they attempt to create a dignified life. Many use hip hop to re-create their colonized spaces and turn them into places. The most obvious reclaiming or reterritorialization of urban space by these Chican@ youth is the vibrant, beautiful hip hop graffiti and murals seen wherever Chican@ youth live and move. For many the extremely loud, bass-heavy music coming out of stylized vehicles is cause for alarm and an indication of social breakdown. When seen from the perspective of reterritorialization, however, the loud music becomes a means for claiming and occupying space. Young people who have little to no legal claim to space use cultural expression to temporarily liberate space from corporate and state control (Alvarez 2008). While these mobile temporary autonomous zones do not directly challenge the State nor the colonial condition, they do provide temporary reprieve from State violence and inspire feelings of dignity. The esteem and positive self-evaluation that expressive culture and reterritorialization provide not only improve the psychic and spiritual lives of the colonized but also are a prerequisite for any social change action (Piven and Cloward 1978). In order to make claims of justice or autonomy, one must feel worthy. Piven and Cloward (4) show us that the emergence of 'poor people's movements' comes from a change in consciousness including a belief in the illegitimacy of the system, an end to fatalistic outlooks, and the belief in the possibility that people can change a system. Decolonial theorists argue similarly. Coulthard (2014, 43) citing Fanon writes, "the colonized must initiate the process of decolonization by first recognizing themselves as free, dignified, and distinct contributors to humanity . . . struggle for freedom on their own terms and in accordance with their own values." Dignity is a prerequisite for revolutionary alterNative action. Like the Zapatistas who elevated dignity to the status of revolutionary praxis for indigenous people, Chican@ street hop artists "try to change the status quo by imagining a community with dignity" (Peláez Rodriguez 2016, 196).

A Third Space Chicana Street Hop

Men and masculine perspectives dominate the street hop genre like hip hop more generally. Like their Xicano hip hop brethren, they mostly stay away from the misogynist and the homophobic found in popular corporate-controlled rap but women's voices are largely absent from street hop and complex representations of women and women's perspectives are few and far between in the music, lyrics, and images of the street hop emcees mentioned above. However, my personal introduction to Chicana street hop came as a result of Krazy Race's efforts to highlight great women emcees including some Chicanas. His and MC Nejma Shea's compilation two-volume compact disc set *Queens of the Mic* (2011) illustrated a desire on the part of Krazy Race to include a transnational Xicana feminism in his own analysis and within the 'conscious' independent hip hop scene in general.

Tenochtitlan appeared on the *Queens of the Mic* compilation on the tracks, "Sink or Swim" and "Chingonas" with TopDime. This Los Angeles-based Chicana emcee has released a number of songs, been featured on others' songs, and released the full-length compact disc *Obsidian Rapture* in 2011. Her songs express a wide range of emotions, strategies for survival as an indigenous-identified urban Mexican-origin woman, and criticisms of the state of our society. She opens a third space in Chican@ street hop primarily through her empowered autobiographical examinations of herself and her identity. She and TopDime exemplify the Chicana street hop identity on the aforementioned "Chingonas." Rapping in Spanish, English and Chican@ street language or caló, they describe themselves in the chorus as "hermanas chingonas that don't take no shit/hard-ass cabronas/hermosas, preciosas/reinas, diosas poderosas./Soy todas las cosas."

The song and accompanying video is essentially a party anthem. The women emcees celebrate themselves and their friendship. In the video the women get ready to go to a barbecue for a women's night out. They gather all the things they will need to have a good time together including clothes, makeup, marijuana ("I got a tree on a deck"), alcohol, and music. They are preparing for a night of affirming their friendship and identities as urban working-class Chicanas who are powerful or 'chingonas'. They do not get taken advantage of since they "don't take no shit." They are tough street hop women. They are cabronas. They are also beautiful, precious, and princess-like. Additionally, they are goddesses. They are multidimensional subjects.

Tenochtitlan's identity and politics come from being a member of a people or 'nation'. She performs a love letter to her people ("carta de amor para mi pueblo") in "Mi Pueblo." In the first verse of the song she claims an indigenous identity as a "Mexican woman descendant of ancient Aztec kingdom merged with Chicano sistren and brethren." As an indigenous woman she is a "spiritual warrior [who] fight[s] oppression [till] Aztlán is back in our possession." She implores Mexican@s/Chican@s to unite and "walk with ancestors of the fifth sun, Quinto sol." For her Aztlán is not a 'physical territory' but 'financial independence," control of territory and self-determination ("me gente vamos a establecer control").

Imagining an indigenous past and possible Xican@ future, Tenochtitlan furthers her claim to a glorious indigenous existence in the song "1519." The song begins with Mesoamerican flutes and drums that morph seamlessly into hip hop drum sounds. On the first verse she imagines the year 1519 and the beginning of the European invasion of Mexico, or 'predicted cataclysm' as she refers to it. The chorus consists of a sample of a man speaking in Nahuatl over Mesoamerican sounds and ambient sounds of a jungle. Her use of such a landscape attempts to connect Tenochtitlan to her vision of our ancestral past. Her allusions to el Templo Mayor, Aztlán and la diosa Azteca place the 21st-century Chicana emcee within the thousands-years-old indigenous presence in Central and Southern Mexico and the United States Southwest. In the second verse she critiques Chican@s who have "forsaken our ancestors" and attempts to persuade them to see themselves differently than how the dominant U.S. society views them. Chican@s are 'victorious' since we have survived the genocidal onslaught of the continued European invasion or colonialism. Like many of her street hop and Xican@ hip hop colleagues, she hopes to affirm and help develop a sense of pride in her people that would cause them to fight back against colonialism, capitalism, and racism.

Unlike most of her fellow street hop and Xicano hip hop emcees, Tenochtitlan is a woman of Mexican descent in the urban barrios of the United States. As such, she has experiences and perspectives that her male counterparts lack. She, like other female emcees, uses her voice to add a feminist critique to men's anti-state, anti-racist, and anti-capitalist rhetoric. She and TopDime's song "Indominables" exemplifies the Chicana street hop perspective. In the song they rap about rape, prostitution, motherhood, misogyny, and women's uplift. Tenochtitlan opens the song rapping: "looking into my beautiful son and daughter's face/how could I tell them their father was a disgrace?" It turns out that the father left the family, placing them in financial hardship. As a result, they were "living in the dark" and she was "working two jobs to make ends meet." Her drive to protect her children causes her to "choose my children first sacrificing for them to eat." While presented with the incredibly difficult task of raising children by herself, she is able to hold her "head high with dignity."

Similarly to the Zapatistas' call for revolutionary dignity as a basis for and goal of struggle but on a personal level, women like Tenochtitlan's character in the song persevere even under extreme levels of misogynist violence. At the end of the first verse she describes how her character was forced into prostitution. She raps:

> They came and snatched me from the warmth of me bed/kickin and screamin/dragged be down into the twisted realm of sin./What's been done to me could never be forgiven./Eleven year-old virgin sold to grown men/that damaged my hymen, tore me apart, left me bleedin./ I'm fucking ruined./I accept the truth./May god have mercy on this child prostitute.

In other verses on the song, Tenochtitlan and TopDime describe rape and violence and the feelings of desperation and hopelessness that sometimes attend such acts. One character is the wife of a drug dealer from the Tijuana Cartel. She laments the fact that they have money at the risk of potential violence and the suffering of a great number of people.

Their descriptions of different women suffering misogynist violence at the hands of intimate men and strangers helps us see the physical and emotional violence attending colonialism. Colonizers have always raped and otherwise violated native women as a means of warfare against and control of the colonized native. Tenochtitlan and TopDime's narrative of gendered violence remind us that colonialism and capitalism always take place ultimately in the body. We witness this biopower in the rape and beatings described in "Indominables" but also in the attack on our food supply and other means of life as well as the toxic medicines provided by industrial colonial "healthcare."

However, the transnational feminism of Xicana street hop emcees does not allow them to be victims and remain dominated. Instead, they are indominables. They cannot be dominated and they want to encourage this spirit of resistance in other women. The chorus exemplifies their declaration of freedom. They rap:

> Enemies want to take me out, extinguish my life. They're scared to death I may rise, take their piece of the pie. But submission ain't an option no matter the price. For the right to breathe free, I'm ready to die . . . lucharé, esperaré, ganaré. Soy mujer! Hoy declararé mi poder!

Here they claim that misogynist men and other enemies engage in violence against women out of their fear of women's power ("they're scared to death I may rise"). They end the chorus with a rallying cry proclaiming that they will fight, hope, and win because they are women who declare their power. In the final verse they implore other women to adopt their defiant womanness and speak their truths. They perform a lyrical attack on misogyny and the depression and lack of self-worth that often results from it. They rap:

> To all the women of the world, speak the fuck up and let them know you've had enough./No apologies./Fuck that misogyny./Word to my sisters wake up and see clearly why they got you enraged with your self-image./Join me on this feminist/.Stand proud of being female. Fearless./Fuck being depressed and dying obsessed./Take pride in your shit, the sway of your hips, your full lips, built like a goddess.

These Xicanist@ emcees provide a defiant woman-centeredness that sees women outside of patriarchal expectations and the male gaze and offers a third space within hip hop to develop a 21st-century Chican@ identity.

Street Hop's Anti-colonial, Anti-authoritarian AlterNative Potential

As urban racialized targets of the colonial capitalist state, Chican@ street hop emcees have an important but unique critique of the State. While often limited by a liberal reformist influence, Chican@ street hop develops an anti-authoritarian critique similar to that of anarchists in significant ways. Moreover, Chican@ street hop utilizes the celebrated figure of the "outlaw" as a trope for a rebel identity connecting this musical subculture to hundreds of years of Mexican@ and indigenous resistance to oppressive colonial and capitalist economic and legal regimes that limit Xican@ freedom.

Krazy Race's body of work exemplifies the range of critique found in Chican@ street hop. From his early nationalist anthem, "Dedicated," to international politics to discussion of chemtrails, police brutality and imperial warfare, Krazy Race consistently critiques the State from a working-class urban Chicano perspective. Krazy Race's work encapsulates the Chican@ street hop perspective while suggesting a more radical direction for street hop that includes a Chicana third space. Krazy Race's company, Realizm Rekord's, compiled *Queens of the Mic*, the two-disc anthology of women emcees. This two-disc set, perhaps more than any other, highlights independent street hop women of color. MC Nejma Shea's collaboration with Krazy Race models how independent street hop artists can work across boundaries of gender, race, and sexuality to provide high-quality progressive music.

Street hop and Chican@ hip hop more generally have great potential as decolonial aesthetics given the working class/underclass, gendered, and racialized experiences of its practitioners. Chican@ street hop generally lacks a female space and is a less-than-welcoming environment for GLBTQ2 and jot@s. In addition, its effectiveness as a decolonial art that can help us develop a broad-based anti-authoritarian, anti-colonial, alterNative perspective depends on whether street hop can ally with the politically active sectors of their community. What role might Chican@ street hop and Xican@ hip hop play in a broad anti-colonial movement alongside people like the water protectors who fight the destruction of native land and vital resources including and especially water, the Zapatistas and their global network, anti-fascist networks, the prison abolition movement, anti-state violence organizations, and the global movement against capitalism and imperialism?

Notes

1 See groups and individual performers such as Psycho Realm, Thief Sicario, Sick Symphonies, Krazy Race, Juan Zarate, and Sicko Soldado for excellent examples of street hop using the loco episteme.
2 Olguín alerts us to this tendency and warns against seeing pint@ culture as positively resistant. The Zapatistas and their spokesperson, Subcommandante Marcos (2002), Alvarez (2008), and hooks (2001) all provide important examinations of revolutionary love and dignity.

Bibliography

Alexander, Michelle. 2012. *The New Jim Crow: Mass Incarceration in the Age of Colorblindness*. New York: The New Press.

Alvarez, Luis. 2008. *The Power of the Zoot: Youth Culture and Resistance During World War II*. Berkeley: University of California Press.

Coulthard, G. S. 2014. *Red Skin, White Masks: Rejecting the Colonial Politics of Recognition*. Minneapolis: University of Minnesota Press.

Davis, Angela. 2003. *Are Prisons Obsolete?* New York: Seven Stories Press.

Dunbar-Ortiz, Roxanne. 2015. *An Indigenous Peoples' History of the United States*. Boston: Beacon Press.

Flores Magón, Ricardo. 2005. *Dreams of Freedom: A Ricardo Flores Magón Reader*. Oakland, CA: AK Press.

hooks, bell. 2001. *All About Love: New Visions*. New York: William Morrow.

McFarland, Pancho. 2013. *The Chican@ Hip Hop Nation: Politics of a New Millennial Mestizaje*. East Lansing: Michigan State University Press.

MC Nejma Shea and Krazy Race. 2011. *Queens of the Mic*. Realizm Rekords.

Mirandé, Alfredo. 1987. *Gringo Justice*. Notre Dame: University of Notre Dame Press.

Olguín, Ben V. 2010. *La Pinta: Chicana/o Prisoner Literature, Culture, and Politics*. Austin: University of Texas Press.

Paredes, Americo. 1958. *With His Pistol in His Hand: A Border Ballad and Its Hero*. Austin: University of Texas Press.

Parenti, Christian. 2000. *Lockdown America: Police and Prisons in the Age of Crisis*. London: Verso.

Peláez Rodríguez, Diana C. 2016. "Chicana Hip Hop: Expanding Knowledge in the L.A. Barrio." In Castillo-Garsow, Melissa and Jason Nichols (eds.). *La Verdad: An International Dialogue on Hip Hop Latinidades*. Columbus: Ohio State University Press. Pp. 183–202.

Piven, Frances Fox and Richard Cloward. 1978. *Poor People's Movements: Why They Succeed, How They Fail*. New York: Vintage.

Psycho Realm. www.psychorealm.com.

Subcommandante Marcos. 2002. *Our Word Is Our Weapon: Selected Writings*. New York: Seven Stories.

Tenochtitlan. 2010. *Obsidian Rapture.*

Villa, Raul Homero. 2000. *Barrio Logos: Space and Place in Urban Chicano Literature and Culture*. Austin: University of Texas Press.

Zarate, Juan. (2008). *El Sacrificio* (album).

5 Expanding Chican@ Hip Hop Anti-colonialism

Identity matters. Understanding the current political, economic, cultural, spiritual, and social worlds requires examination of how we define ourselves and how we are defined by others. How we define ourselves and the source information/experiences upon which this definition is made tell us a great deal about ourselves and our world. How Chican@s define themselves and are defined provides important insight into our society. When the subaltern Chican@ speaks, whether pinto poet, emcee, scholar, or organic intellectual, we experience a counter-narrative to the official mythology of our nation. The voices of Xican@ emcees offer an 'epistemic decolonization' central to any real revolutionary change. Enrique Dussel argues that "many 'leftist' movements have failed the people because they have not engaged in 'a decolonization of philosophy, science" (Dussel and Hernandez 2016). Dussel, like indigenous anti-colonial theorists discussed previously, sees a return to and development of indigenous philosophy as the key to developing a significant anti-colonial praxis. The study of Chican@ street hop and Xican@ hip hop offers a useful example of how some interrogate meaning, identity, race, nation, the United States, and our late capitalist world.

The narratives told by the subaltern Chican@ emcee illustrate two common identities that connect this generation of artists to previous generations of storytellers. The pinto/outlaw and the indigenous warrior have long histories in Chican@ artistic expression. The question for social justice advocates is how do these identities and the politics that accompany them contribute to a liberatory praxis. What role can these identities play in forging a more fair, just, equitable, and free world? How can they be put in the service of a 'better' world? What role does an anti-colonial aesthetics play in an anti-colonial movement?

Essentialist understandings of identity including various forms of nationalism have been problematic. Comparing the indigenous-based nationalism of much of Chican@ poetics to Europeanized nationalisms, Arteaga points out that while the indigenous nationalism is a response to the terror imposed by foreign European regimes, they still are limiting. Arteaga (1997, 146) warns that indigenous identity amongst Chican@s can be problematic since they imagine that Chican@ "subjectivity descended from one source." While indigenous identities have different ramifications, especially as regards potential for decolonization, relative to "Mexican American," "Latin@," or "Hispanic" identity, it often remains "idealized" and "unitary." Along similar lines of critique, Contreras's (2008) reading of Chican@ indigenous literature shows how much of the Chican@ indigenous identity was constructed from questionable colonial-era sources and with romantic nostalgia. Romantic indigenism on the part of some Chican@s replaces one colonial master ('White' men) with another (Aztec kings). For the most part, Marxist and anarchist scholars and activists reject most forms of nationalism and other forms of identitarian politics as reactionary forms of false consciousness used by the ruling class to divide the working class.

Indigenous and anti-colonial scholars disagree with the typical Marxist and anarchist anti-nationalism and fetishizing of the working class as the only revolutionary identity. They reject the focus on class as the proper conceptual basis for understanding the problems of indigenous people and people of color. Rather, the key power dynamic is native-colonizer. As such, decolonization is the means and indigenous renewal is the end. In Ramnath's (2011, 21) insightful 'decolonization of anarchism' she offers a useful means of understanding decolonialism: it is "restoring the artificially stunted capacity to freely grow and evolve without forcible outside interference to constrict the space of potential." It is about self-determination. In order to be self-determined and self-identified indigenous people, traditional lands are required. Marxists, anarchists, and other Eurocentric radicals misunderstand how indigenous identity is connected to community and place. Thus, a revolutionary subjectivity for indigenous people cannot be an abstract working class but rather a place-based community or national identity.

Nationalism for the colonized and indigenous responds to the colonial attack on identity and indigenous being including and especially dispossession from traditional lands and, thus, cultural practices. Indigenous anti-colonial nationalism is defined by community responsibility for the land and all our relations. It is anti-state, does not rely on private property, and does not demand "exclusive control over territory" (Smith 2011, 60). Indigenous nationalisms challenge the capitalist colonialist claim to territory by rejecting private property and ownership and invoking knowledge of place and adherence to natural laws of a territory. Thus, indigenous nationalism is not based on individual property rights but "on a system of interrelatedness and mutual responsibility" (Smith 2011, 58).

While Xican@ hip hop emcees offer an anti-colonialism in their art, an honest analysis of the pinto/outlaw tradition and its latest iteration as

Chican@ street hop offers a warning to evaluate the art critically, complexly, and completely. Prison and street culture and its expression resist and rebel against certain aspects of our society and its institutions. However as Olguín (2010, 15) explains: "These crime subcultures are not always empowering and, to be honest, rarely revolutionary. On the contrary, crime-as-subaltern agency can be as repressive as, and integral to, colonial domination." The criminalization of popular culture, especially gangsta rap and corporate rap, continues the ideological domination of the settler-colonial state and its capitalist beneficiaries. Ball (2011, 51) explains that "the popularization of a narrowly constructed form of hip-hop is part of the colonizing process that supports the continued and necessary devolution of African America." Chican@s as indigenous people suffer the same kind of indoctrination. Moreover, settler-colonial capitalism rewards Chican@s and other colonized or racialized people who through their art popularize this narrow view of indigenous people and people of color. Few rewards, if any, are accrued to those like Xican@ and street hop emcees who offer more complex, even revolutionary, anti-colonial perspectives. The "crime-as-subaltern agency" perspective found in some Chicano hip hop texts reflects the system of rewards established by colonial capitalism. Moreover, the more politically conscious Chican@ street hop risks devolving into gangsta chic and reactionary violence when it vies for a portion of the hundreds of millions of dollars made from speaking about fratricidal violence in hip hop.

Chican@ hip hop expresses a great deal of agency as the performers challenge the social arrangements that cause barrioization. Their critiques of the State and capital are often prescient (McFarland 2013). Yet, the critique fails to account for other aspects and expressions of power including hypermasculinity, homophobia, heteronormativity, and interpersonal violence. The relative lack of female voices in Chican@ hip hop vividly makes the point about the masculinist worldview in which the subculture operates. When women speak in hip hop they often challenge the masculinist assumptions and structures that limit its empowering possibilities.

Pan-Indigenous Transnationalism

A Xican@ hip hop anti-colonialism would necessarily be transnational. It would be aware and concerned for all oppressed people and would fight for the overthrow of capitalism and colonialism while doing the difficult work of reclaiming our identities and dignidad. Given the similar conditions that indigenous people have faced since Columbus's fated arrival, a pan-indigenous movement has developed in which indigenous peoples throughout the Americas and in other parts of the world develop a common identity as indigenous and resistant. Xican@ hip hop artists do well when they more fully incorporate this movement into their analyses, participate in it, and engage in solidarity with other indigenous people across the planet. Equally any analysis such as that found in this study must also seriously engage indigenous perspectives beyond the United States. The following is a small sample of non-Xican@ indigenous hip hop.

Non-Xican@ Indigenous hip hop groups and solo performers utilize the same imagery and ideas as the Xican@ hip hop emcees mentioned throughout this study. Groups such as the Tihorappers Crew from Quintana Roo, Mexico extend our analysis from the United States to the center of Mayan culture (Villegas 2016). The members of the Crew look and move like any number of other young brown hip hop headz. They use hip hop beats and other hip hop musical characteristics while, like Xicano emcees, they speak about dignity, identity, tradition, politics, and fun. In addition, like most in hip hop, they use multiple idioms including Mayan languages, Spanish, and hip hop phrases to make their points.

The group Linaje Originarios, consisting of two cousins, Brayan and Dario Tascón, hails from Colombia and uses hip hop as a means of preserving their language and culture. They rap in the language of Emberá and use Spanish occasionally. Their use of Emberá illustrates indigenous pride but also has the important practical goal of preserving Emberá culture and their endangered language, of which there are only approximately 80,000 speakers (Molandes 2016). The videos for their songs "Hijos Indígenas," "Condor Pasa," and "Raperos Indígenas Por la Paz" illustrate their concern for the preservation of their traditions and about state violence against indigenous people. They film their videos using images of their natural surroundings, suggesting the connection between indigenous identity, land, and all our relations; depict rituals and dance; and dress in traditional clothing as well as hip hop styles. Their body movements and music are puro hip hop, demonstrating the hybrid/mestizo nature of contemporary indigenous hip hop youth. On "Condor Pasa" they use traditional pan flutes and stringed instruments playing the Andean song as the melody and musical foundation, as well as utilize the standard boom-boom bap beat, expressive high hat rhythms, and other hip hop musical elements. The video opens with images of purification and other rituals, traditional beading practices, and natural environments.

Linaje Originarios get political on "Raperos Indígenas por la Paz" (Indigenous Rappers for Peace). The video opens with someone painting signs for a peace march with children holding banners and marching to demand an end to war, discrimination, violence, kidnappings, and other injustices that cause susto, which literally means 'fright' but in this context it refers to the numerous illnesses caused by extreme trauma. In Spanish they rap:

> No más Guerra./No más discriminación./No más violencia./No más secuestrarios./Que tan justo ya no tiene gusto./Tanta injusticia que ya ve/esta causando hasta susto./Raperos por la paz./Raperos por la paz./ Hold it down./Hold it down.

In addition, Xican@ emcees would likely agree that an indigenous anti-colonial hip hop analysis would necessarily include non-Xican@ people of native descent from the United States. Native rappers such as Tall Paul, Supaman, Savage Family, and Nataani Means perform hip hop in their indigenous way similar to that of Xican@ emcees. Further, a transnational, pan-indigenous hip hop would include raperos indígenas from places such as Palestine, Africa, and Asia.

A Transnational Queer Hip Hop?

As discussed in Chapter 2, an anti-authoritarian, anti-colonial, alterNative analysis or cultural project such as Xican@ hip hop and street hop must include a decolonization of gender and sexuality and a third space for Xican@s. La jotería and the two-spirited open fourth spaces for an examination of colonialism, anti-colonialism, and ourselves based in the unique experience of the sexually marginalized and gender scorned. Hip hop's homophobia and hypermasculinity is well known. While it is less prominent in 'politically conscious' hip hop, anything out of the heteronorm is ridiculed and used as a metaphor for weakness and degeneracy.

However, like the Xicana emcees who opened up revolutionary third spaces in hip hop and their predecessors in the Chican@ Movement and with the Partido Liberal Mexicano, jot@s, two-spirited, and gay and lesbian Chican@s pry open a fourth space from the margins. Deadlee offers an example of the gay gangsta who identifies with and represents oneself as the ideal heteronormative hypermasculine thug (Rodriguez 2009). However, Deadlee deconstructs the symbolism of heteronormative Chicanismo and the colonial gender system and queers it. He causes us to look twice (at least) before we claim complete understanding of cultural symbols and practices. Like others in la jotería, Deadlee forces us to examine how colonialism and internalized racism use sexuality and masculinity as bludgeons to control colonized populations. Deadlee, in similar fashion as Tenochtitlan, Rain Flowa, and other Xicana emcees and visual artists, shows us how colonialism attacks non-heterosexual and non-male bodies. Their attention to biopower assists us in understanding how anti-colonialism requires a politics of bodily self-determination and integrity, health, physical well-being, and traditional healing and nutritional practices.

Deadlee illustrates how cultural warriors of la jotería provide insight into colonialism and capitalism that anti-colonial scholars and activists can utilize in developing an anti-colonial alterNative analysis. In his song "Good Soldier," he tells the story of a gay Chicano contemplating suicide as a result of trauma induced by colonialist homophobia and the attack on the Brown gay body. Over music featuring an eerie piano pattern and aggressive speed metal drum and guitar punctuations, Deadlee discusses the trauma of coming out to family, a toxic relationship, and masculinity. The young man can no longer be a good soldier, lover, or son. He is fed up with the pretending and taking the insults and violence like a 'good soldier'. He shouts

> I can't be a good soldier. I can't be a good son./I can't be a good lover. I can't be your number one./One night, one gun, one decision./These words resonated over in my head/"I fuckin hate you faggot. Wish you were dead."

On the third verse Deadlee provides a graphic critique of colonialist masculinity, rapping, "cock in my mouth, tongue in some ass./Guess it doesn't fit your definition of a man." He describes gay male sex so that homophobes must confront their hatred and fear. His two-sentence criticism also illustrates how homophobes equate manhood with heterosexuality. Deadlee takes on the violent hypermasculinity of capitalist colonialism and turns a queer mirror on it.

Additionally, Xican@ hip hop anti-colonialism would extend the fourth space transnationally. This expansion might include the Afro-Cuban lesbian hip hop trio, Krudas Cubensi. Like the abovementioned Xicana and queer decolonial focus on biopower, the women of Krudas "favor a radical feminist discourse about the politics of the body and eroticism" (Ramírez 2016, 217). The Afro-Latina queer feminism of Krudas centers the body when discussing colonial and race relations. They dedicate the song "Eres Bella" (2011) to

> todas las mujeres del mundo. Todas las mujeres como nosotras quien estan luchando . . . especialmente la más negra, especialmente la más pobre.
> [all the women of the world. All the women like us who are fighting . . . especially the darkest, especially the poorest.

They rap "artificial straighteners and wigs are/a continuation of the colonialist story/don't get caught up in that, leave that false view behind" (translated in Ramírez 2016). Here Krudas show that "the White hegemony's control of the Black body also includes the subjugation of Black people's hair" (Ramírez 2016, 225). For our purposes in developing a transnational anti-colonial praxis, Krudas Cubensi illustrate an oppositional consciousness and reclamation of an indigenous/African diasporan identity that centers a politics of the body in anti-colonial analysis.

Xican@ Hip Hop and Street Hop's AlterNative Analysis

This study asks whether there is an anti-colonial aesthetics in the hip hop culture of people of Mexican descent in the United States. To what degree can the aesthetics and narratives of Xican@ hip hop and street hop contribute to a broader revolutionary analysis of our current political economic situation and inspire Xican@s, other indigenous people, and oppressed people to decolonize and re-indigenize? What role does place and identity have in developing an anti-colonial praxis? In Chapter 2 I offered a synthesis of anarchist, indigenous, transnational feminist, and la jotería/two-spirited studies as an anti-authoritarian, anti-colonial, alterNative framework for determining whether and to what degree people of Mexican descent in hip hop provide a liberatory analysis. My framework consists of the following traits:

anti-capitalist	anti-State	anti-industrial	anti-hierarchical
anti-misogynist	place-based	participatory	decentralized
gender fluid	communal	inclusive of all our relations	

While the hip hop under investigation in this study falls short of some of the above, it does challenge the State, capitalism, and industrialism. It encourages anti-hierarchical thinking and professes place, community, and democracy. Xican@ hip hop, more than street hop, uses indigenous practices such as decentralization, mitakuye oyasin (all my relations), community focus and place as a means for its identity and politics. The third spaces and fourth spaces opened by women and la jotería, two-spirited, and gays and lesbians promise to challenge hip hop's misogyny, homophobia, and queerphobia.

The promise of an anti-colonial aesthetics is in its ability to move people and be a part of a movement that is not merely symbolic and aesthetic but engages in anti-colonial struggle. The peril is that like all revolutionary culture and practice, the profound analyses of Xican@ emcees can easily be commodified. Their honoring of the Earth, our elders, ancestors and all our relations can become the next mass-marketed 'radical' commodity such as Malcom X hats, Black Panther Party-inspired revolutionary chic, or leather 'Africa' medallions. The artists must work and live within the confines of capitalist colonialism. In order to spread their anti-colonial aesthetics, they must sell their music, get 'hits' on social media outlets, and sell merchandise. The lure of money for survival if not luxury tends to soften the message. Hip hop icon and mogul, Jay-Z, explained the problem well in his song "Moment of Clarity" from his 2003, *The Black Album*:

> I dumbed down for my audience to double my dollars./They criticized me for it, yet they all yell 'holla'./If skills sold, truth be told, I'd probably be lyrically Talib Kweli./Truthfully I wanna rhyme like Common Sense/but I did 5 mil./I ain't been rhyming like Common since . . . We, as rappers, must decide what's most important/and I can't help the poor if I'm one of them./So, I got rich and gave back. To me that's the win-win.

Here the highly influential multi-millionaire explains that it is through participation in the capitalist economic system that he can be of best service to poor people. In his mind, philanthropy is the best bet for bringing people out of poverty. He explains this capitalist logic further by invoking the well-respected lyricists, Talib Kweli and Common (fka Common Sense), who are known for their lyrical challenges to racism, ecological destruction, and capitalism and their pro-Black messages of uplift. However, neither of them has made the kind of money or had the kind of influence that Jay-Z has had with his paeans to capitalism, consumerism, and 'street life'. So, Jay-Z chose sales over dignity, uplift, and revolutionary critique. To what degree can we expect the same out of Xican@ emcees? Will in lak 'ech buttons and bumper stickers be the apex of Xican@ hip hop rebellion? If not, what type of revolutionary anti-authoritarian, anti-colonial alterNative can Xican@ emcees inspire or engage in?

My challenge to the hip hop, activist, and scholarly communities is to ask how we can expand the liberatory possibilities of hip hop. The success of a social movement depends on the degree to which its message resonates with a mass public. How can we assist Xican@ hip hop, street hop, and anti-colonial actors distribute their understanding to more people? Can indigenous anti-colonial thought and anti-colonial aesthetics including Xican@ hip hop provide a foundation upon which to build a mass movement? I sense that through deeper engagement between revolutionary anti-colonial actors and anti-colonial cultural practitioners, the resistance and recovery offered by hip hop will become more profound and will inspire more people with the alterNative message of dignidad. Importantly, as I have tried to suggest, Xican@ hip hop and street hop need to engage doubly and triply oppressed Xican@s and indigenous people including women and GLBTQ2 members of our communities to reach their anti-authoritarian, anti-colonial alterNative potential.

Bibliography

Arteaga, Alfred. 1997. *Chicano Poetics: Heterotexts and Hybridities*. Cambridge: Cambridge University Press.

Ball, Jared A. 2011. *I Mix What I Like: A Mixtape Manifesto*. Oakland, CA: AK Press.

Contreras, Sheila. 2008. *Bloodlines*. Austin: University of Texas Press.

Deadlee. 2009. "Good Soldier." www.youtube.com/watch?v=FmzrO1HyCWw.

Dussel, Ernesto and C. Hernandez. 2016. "Enrique Dussel: Without Epistemic Decolonization, There Is No Revolution." *La Iguana*. October 21, 2016. Downloaded from Venezuela Analysis.com. https://venezuelanalysis.com/analysis/12734.

Jay-Z. 2003. *The Black Album*. Roc-A-Fella Records.

Las Krudas. 2013. "Bio." www.krudascubensi.com/.

Linaje Originario. 2016. "El Condor Pasa." www.youtube.com/watch?v=8Q68w Bc4naQ.

McFarland, Pancho. 2013. *The Chican@ Hip Hop Nation: Politics of a New Millennial Mestizaje*. East Lansing: Michigan State University Press.

Molandes, Lucas. 2016. "These Cousins Are Rapping in Their Indigenous Language to Preserve Their Culture." *Mitú*. www.wearemitu.com/mitu-world/these-cousins-are-rapping-in-their-indigenous-language-to-preserve-their-culture. September 6.

Olguín, Ben V. 2010. *La Pinta: Chicana/o Prisoner Literature, Culture, and Politics*. Austin: University of Texas Press.

Ramírez, Sandra Abd'allah-Alvarez. 2016. "Conscious Cuban Rap: Krudas Cubensi and Supercrónica Obsesión." In Castillo-Garsow, Melissa and Jason Nichols (eds.). *La Verdad: An International Dialogue on Hip Hop Latinidades*. Columbus: Ohio State University Press. Pp. 214–227.

Ramnath, Maia. 2011. *Decolonizing Anarchism*. Oakland, CA: AK Press.

Rodriguez, Richard T. 2009. *Next of Kin: The Family in Chicano/a Cultural Politics*. Durham, NC: Duke University Press.

Smith, Andrea. 2011. "Queer Theory and Native Studies: The Heteronormativity of Settler Colonialism." In Driskill, Q., C. Finle, B. J. Gilley, and S. L. Morgensen (eds.). *Queer Indigenous Studies: Critical Interventions in Theory, Politics, and Literature*. Tucson: University of Arizona Press. Pp. 43–65.

Tihorappers Crew. "Facebook page." www.facebook/tihorapperscrew.

Villegas, Omar. 2016. "There's a Crew in Mexico Rapping in Maya." *Mitu*. www.wearemitu.com/mitu-world/a-group-of-mexican-rappers-are-making-music-to-instill-pride-in-their-community. September 30.

Index